52
SIMPLE WAYS
TO · MAKE
CHRISTMAS SPECIAL

52 SIMPLE WAYS TO·MAKE CHRISTMAS SPECIAL

Jan Dargatz

OLIVER NELSON

A Division of Thomas Nelson Publishers

NASHVILLE

Published in Nashville, Tennessee, by Oliver-Nelson Books, a division of Thomas Nelson, Inc., Publishers, and distributed in Canada by Lawson Falle, Ltd., Cambridge, Ontario.

Unless otherwise noted, the Bible version used in this publication is THE NEW KING JAMES VERSION. Copyright © 1979, 1980, 1982, Thomas Nelson, Inc., Publishers.

Scripture quotations marked NIV are taken from the HOLY BIBLE: NEW INTERNATIONAL VERSION. Copyright © 1973, 1978, 1984 by the International Bible Society. Used by permission of Zondervan Bible Publishers.

Printed in the United States of America.

Library of Congress Cataloging-in-Publication Data
Dargatz, Jan Lynette.
    52 simple ways to make this Christmas special / Jan Dargatz.
        p.   cm.
    ISBN 0-8407-9596-3 (pbk.)
    1. Christmas.   2. Advent.   3. Epiphany.   I. Title.   II. Title:
    Fifty-two simple ways to make this Christmas special.
    GT4985.D435   1991
    394.2′68282—dc20   91-11413
                                                                         CIP

1   2   3   4   5   6   —   96   95   94   93   92   91

Dedicated to

Craig

my beloved brother
and favorite childhood
Christmas coconspirator

★ Contents

★ Introduction

Christmas is not just a day. It is a full *season* with three traditional parts:

- The sober, reflective, preparatory time of *Advent,* which comes twenty-one to twenty-eight days before Christmas Day. It is during this time that the Church, traditionally, has prepared itself for the coming of Jesus the Christ: His past coming as a squalling infant into the dark grotto of a Bethlehem stable; His future coming as King of kings and Lord of lords, the Messiah who will rule and reign forever; and His present coming into our individual lives and our church communities as living Lord, Redeemer, Savior, Healer, Deliverer, and ever-present Friend of friends.

- The grand celebration of *Christmastide,* the twelve days beginning with Christmas Day. It is during this time that Christians around the world have traditionally "made merry" with joyous abandon. Christmastide is a time for family and friends, for singing and feasting, for sending greetings and hosting parties. It is a time for rejoicing that heaven has struck a path all the way to the very gates of hell and has invited every human being to walk upon it toward everlasting life.

- *Epiphany,* January 6, the day that the Church commemorates the arrival of the wise men from the East bearing their precious gifts of gold, frankincense, and myrrh. It is a day traditionally associated with gift giving, a day for reflecting upon the Gift of gifts from a heavenly Father to a needy world. Many of us have combined the gift giving of Epiphany with the celebration of Christmas Day.

The three facets of the Christmas season have a wonderful harmony to them. The sober, reflective, quiet days of Advent give way to the glorious light and merriment of Christmas, and out of a spirit of joy and thanksgiving, gifts flow naturally.

In our culture today, the three seasons of Christmas seem to have become a little muddled. Our children often await Santa Claus more than the birth of the Christ child. We put up our Christmas trees just after Thanksgiving and take them down the day after Christmas rather than putting them up on Christmas Eve and enjoying them until Epiphany. We delight in the bustle and parties before Christmas Day and then wonder why we feel a little depressed and lonely in the days that follow it. By New Year's Day, the party seems to be over. We begin the new year in debt, dread taking down the lights on the house and bushes outside, resolve to embark on major life changes, and often harbor a lingering feeling of unfulfillment.

52 Simple Ways to Make Christmas Special is a challenge to return to tradition. It calls for Advent to be a personal advent, Christmastide to be a celebration, and Epiphany to be a glorious conclusion to the holiday season. This book provides ideas, loosely grouped, for each facet of the season. Suggestions for spiritual reflection are grouped in the Advent section, ideas for celebration in the Christmas section, and hints for giving in the Epiphany section.

Truly it is a marvel that we commemorate Christmas year after year after year. If Christmas were only a time of commercialized gift giving, we might have let it run its course years ago. No, our souls *need* Christmas. We have a deep human need to call attention to the origin of our faith on a periodic basis, to become aware once again that God reached down and extended to the earth His love incarnate. We need a starting-over point for our inner lives, a time for renewal, rededication, and rejoicing. Christmas is something we cannot do without.

Therefore, let's make Christmas even more special. Let's delight in it to the fullest! Let's mark the holidays as holy days. In so doing, we will find more meaning, more fulfillment, and more joy.

ADVENT

A Season for Reflection

1 ★ Make a Decision to Keep Advent in Your Heart

Sacred infant, all divine,
What a tender love was thine,
Thus to come from highest bliss
Down to such a world as this.
                    —Winter's Snow

Advent marks the beginning of the church calendar, the turning over of the liturgy to the starting point of a new church year.

A new beginning is only that if you choose to make it so. There is nothing inherently special about New Year's Day. It is just another dawn and dusk as nature plays its hand. New Year's Day is special because we have declared it to be so. The same holds true for Advent. Advent is a special time of new beginning only because you choose to make it so in your heart.

Advent is the ideal time to make spiritual decisions. The scripture lessons of Advent include the words of John the Baptist as he quotes from the prophet Isaiah: "Prepare the way of the LORD,/Make His paths straight" (Matt. 3:3). Advent is a time of:

- *preparation,*

- *expectation,*

- *anticipation,*

- *waiting.*

Advent is a time for facing one's sins and repenting of them. Take time during the weeks before Christmas to pray in the spirit of the saints of the past: "Create in me a clean heart, O God,/And renew a steadfast spirit within me." (Ps. 51:10).

Advent is a time for making spiritual resolutions. What new discipline is the Lord prompting you to keep in your life? What new avenue of service is He opening up to you? What new level of giving are you feeling led to enter? List them. Reflect upon your answers and your resolutions related to them.

Advent is a time for expecting the good things of God. What good thing is it that you desire the Lord to do for you? in you? through you? What blessings do you desire to receive from His hand? Write them down.

Advent is a time for anticipating the Lord's return to the earth. What will this earth be like under the rule and reign of Jesus? No more sickness. No more war. No more sorrow or despair. No more poverty.

Advent is a time for waiting in the Lord's presence. Set aside a time each day to sit in His presence. Think of the good things that the Lord has done for you. Quietly praise Him for them. *Wait* on the Lord. Let His peace fill the hollow void in your life. Allow His presence to enter in and satisfy.

2 ★ Keep an Advent Calendar

Come, thou long-expected Jesus,
Born to set thy people free;
From our fears and sins release us,
Let us find our rest in thee.
—Come, Thou Long-Expected Jesus

Advent calendars aren't just for children. They are for entire families, for parents, for single adults, for *you*! An Advent calendar helps put your focus on the reason for the season. By opening one of its little windows each day, you will have a renewed awareness of the passing of time, the days drawing ever closer to Christmas Eve.

Purchase an Advent Calendar   Many people, including many Christians, have never seen or used an Advent calendar. To you I say, "Try one!" Beautiful Advent calendars are available for purchase in many bookstores or department stores. The calendars are generally of winter or holiday scenes with numbered panels or doors that open to reveal pictures behind them. One panel is to be opened each day, in sequence, from the beginning of Advent to Christmas. Other calendars are three-dimensional and have little gifts, candies, or ornaments hidden behind their windows as part of the calendar's scene. The final symbol, ornament, or picture is usually that of the baby Jesus lying in a manger. An Advent calendar builds to that moment, the coming of the Lord.

A number of Advent calendars reveal symbols behind their panels—bells, stars, lambs, and so forth. These symbols are generally related to the Christmas story in some way. Establish "opening the door" on the calendar as a regular part of your daily routine during Advent.

Encourage your child to keep an Advent notebook, drawing his or her own version of the symbol or the object behind the panel and then writing something about it.

Make Your Own Calendar   You may want to make your own Advent calendar. This can be a fun activity for Thanksgiving Day while dinner is cooking or after the meal when everyone is ready for a quiet time.

First, prepare two pieces of paper identical in size and shape. Your advent calendar doesn't need to be square or rectangular. You may want to make one in the shape of a star or an evergreen tree. You will want a calendar that is at least 8½" by 11" and preferably 11" by 14".

Next, help your child mark out the panels and perforate three sides of each one with a pin. You will need to make as many panels as there are days between the start of Advent and Christmas. (When in doubt, start your Advent calendar with December 1 and have 24 panels.) The panels don't all need to be the same size; some can be larger than others.

Put the two pieces of paper together as you perforate so that the pin pricks on the top sheet show through onto the second piece of paper underneath.

Then let your child draw a Christmas picture of his own creation on the top sheet of paper. As he does, carefully outline the boxes made by the pin pricks on the second sheet.

Discuss various symbols with your child and let your child draw those symbols in the boxes on the second sheet. Make one of the panels a place to put a picture of the baby Jesus. You may want to cut this from one of last year's Christmas cards. You might also just write the name JESUS in that panel. Be sure to mark on the *top* sheet of paper—the one on which your child is coloring a larger scene—the location of that final panel. Glue the two sheets together (around the edges only).

The final step is to put numbers on the three-sided panels on the top drawing. Use a contrasting color or dark ink. (The numbers should be small and not distract from the overall scene.) Place the numbers at random, if you so desire, but make certain that the panel designated for December 24 is the one with the baby Jesus behind it.

An Advent calendar is also a reminder to yourself and a way to point out to your child that the real meaning of Christmas isn't what we see, taste, or experience in the world. We celebrate Christmas by remembering that Jesus desires to be born anew in our hearts, minds, and souls.

3 ★ Keep an Advent Diary

O come, thou Wisdom from on high,
And order all things far and nigh;
To us the path of knowledge show
And cause us in her ways to go.
— O Come, O Come Emmanuel

An Advent diary is an excellent way to record your reflections, hopes, and prayers during the Advent season.

- You may want to keep the diary active from year to year, making only a few entries each season.

- You may want to have a diary for just one year. You can add entries for Christmastide and Epiphany to encompass the full scope of the holiday season.

- You may want to create a family Advent diary, inviting each member of your family to make entries.

- You may want to illustrate your diary with cutouts from favorite Christmas cards.

- You may want to invite each of your children to keep a Christmas diary. Encourage your child to record her favorite memories, her Christmas prayer list, perhaps even a letter to the baby Jesus.

- You may want to include mementos of the holiday season in your Advent diary—a sprig of pressed holly, a program from a special event, a photograph or sketch of a winter scene.

Personal   *Keep your diary personal.* Let this be a place where you express yourself in a private, intimate way. Use your diary as a mean of recording:

- your insights into the Christmas story and the Advent season;

- your spiritual longings and desires;

- your hopes and expectations for what Christ will accomplish in and through your life; and

- your reflections on the symbols of the season.

Christ-Centered   *Keep your diary Christ-centered.* You may find yourself feeling at odds with the materialism and commercialism around you. You may be feeling lonely or disappointed at dreams and hopes unfulfilled, or perhaps you are feeling a little sad as you experience long winter nights and short colder days. Express your thoughts in terms of what Christ means to you *in that feeling.* What does it mean for Jesus to be born in the midst of the stable of your loneliness? What does it mean for Jesus to arrive in the crowded bustle of your overstuffed holiday agenda?

Your entries in an Advent diary need not be long. They may be only a few words. Your entries need not be world-class prose or poetry. They need only be genuine expressions from your heart. Indeed, Advent is a time for letting your heart feel the heartbeat of the Lord.

4 ★ Take a Winter Nature Walk

Tell us ye birds, why come ye here,
Into this stable, poor and drear?
Hast'ning we seek the newborn King,
And all our sweetest music bring.
— Whence Comes This Rush of Wings?

Bundle up, put on your boots, and go out for a walk. Experience winter. Allow yourself to delight in it.

During the holiday season, most of us adults rush to get from place of warmth to place of warmth, from indoors to indoors. We hurry from house to car to church, from taxi to store to taxi to home, from work to bus to home. We brace ourselves against the bitter sting of winter's cold and delight in holding a cup of warm beverage while putting our stockinged toes up to be toasted by a roaring fire.

Be a child for a day or an afternoon or an evening. Get out there and *feel* winter.

Snow

- Notice your own footsteps as you walk through the snow. Pause to notice the smooth sculpture of snow drifts. Make "smoke" rings as you exhale into the frosty air. Look at the bare trees. Watch the birds that fly in winter. Keep an eye out for animal tracks.

- Listen for the sounds of winter—the crackle of ice, the crunch of your own footsteps through the snow.

- Smell the smoke coming from your neighbors' fireplaces as you walk down your street. Crush up a handful of evergreen needles from a tree or bush and savor the aroma.

- Build a snowman.

- Taste the falling snowflakes.

- Stare into the night sky.

- And if you are really daring, lie down on your back and wave your arms and legs to make your own snow angel!

Sand   Do you live where it is warm? Go for a walk along the beach at night. Look at your footsteps in the cold sand; count the shades of gray in the waves.

Whatever the landscape of your winter, *let your imagination soar.* Can you see the sky filled with angels singing "glory to God in the highest"? Can you hear the sound of children's laughter as their sleds race down the hill? Or close your eyes and imagine children using sleds to ride the ocean's waves? Imagine a palm tree decorated for Christmas. Envision the barren trees once again green. Can you hear a spring robin sing?

Through the eyes of a child, see the full potential of winter. It is perhaps with that same vision that our heavenly Father saw this world.

5 ★ Have Your Own Silent Night

Silent night, holy night,
All is calm, all is bright.
　　　　　—Silent Night

Create a silent night just for yourself. If your house is filled with family, your silent night may need to fall during the wee morning hours. Or, send the children out with your spouse for an evening of Christmas shopping. You may even opt for a "silent dawn."

Quiet Time Whatever time you choose to carve out for yourself, create a space of at least an hour in which you, and you alone, can delight in your own decorations, your own celebration of the season, your own quiet time of reflection, praise, and prayer.

- Put on your favorite Christmas music.

- Build a fire in the fireplace or create a "fireplace" with an array of candles.

- Pour yourself a tall glass of eggnog or your favorite Christmas beverage.

- Turn off all the lights in the room, leaving only the Christmas tree lights.

- Sit back and relax in the moment.

Really listen to the words of the carols and the songs that you have chosen to play. Stare deeply into the flames. Watch the play of light and shadows around the room. Sip your drink slowly.

Choose to smile. Reflect on those things that give cause for your heart to feel joy. For what are you thankful? In what do you feel blessed?

Prayer Time In the calm of your night, give voice to your prayers. You may find yourself whispering. You may find yourself voicing your prayers as single words— "health," "peace," "restoration," "forgiveness." Perhaps your prayer will be just a quiet litany of the names of those you love. You may find yourself shrouded in quiet holiness, awed and even overwhelmed by His presence. Allow your prayer to be what it will be, not necessarily what you have always said or done as prayer. Allow your heart to take you on a new path in His presence.

If at all possible, let the music play until it ends. Let the candles burn themselves out. Let the fire reduce itself to coals. Tip your glass to enjoy the last drop. In the rush and bustle and noise of the holiday season, how important it is to turn down the volume of our lives . . . and listen.

6 ★ Embark on an Early Advent Fast

By this lowly birth of mine,
Sinner, riches shall be thine,
Matchless gifts and free;
Willingly this yoke I take,
And this sacrifice I make,
Heaping joys for thee.
—Noble

The holiday season is often synonymous with gluttony. Not only do we overeat but we usually overdo everything: drinks, decorations, tight schedules, relatives and friends, and extravagant gifts. We have come to *expect* to be overextended in every dimension during the holiday season. And often, we feel overwrought by our own overdoing!

Advent is a good time to chart an alternate course:

- *Shut off the input.*

- *Shut down the systems of our lives.*

- *And, shut ourselves away, even if it's just for a day.*

What Kinds of Fasts   An early Advent fast may very well be a fasting from food. Consider setting aside at least a day for limiting your intake to water or unsweetened fruit juices. Allow your body a moment of respite; consider this to be a time for a cleansing for your physical system.

You may want to fast from morning to night for several days. You may choose to limit your intake to certain types of foods (preferably fruits and vegetables that are fresh and mostly water). Or set aside the entire Advent season as a time for abstaining from liquor, sugar, or high-fat foods.

If you are addicted to caffeine, nicotine, or any other chemical substance, Advent is a good season to recognize the hold that these chemicals have over you and to seek help.

You'll want to consult your physician before embarking on any type of fast. Nearly every person, however, can choose to limit her intake or limit his choices as a type of fast.

Why Fast?   Why engage in a physical fast at the start of the holiday season? Apart from the obvious counterattack on weight gain, here are some good reasons:

- A physical fast heightens your sense of taste. It allows you to reenter the world of eating with a new appreciation for the taste of foods, especially the uncombined and unseasoned tastes of fresh fruits and vegetables.

- A physical fast causes your body to feel satisfied with less food. You will likely find that you feel less sluggish.

- A physical fast strengthens your own willpower, giving you a sense of power over your own eating habits.

- A physical fast heightens your other senses, as well as that of taste. Don't be surprised if holiday lights seem brighter to you, the colors of the season enhanced, the smells more vivid, the textures more luxurious.

- Finally, a physical fast heightens the entire Advent feeling of solemnity and reflection. A sparseness of eating is a good accompaniment for starkness of soul.

If you must indulge, let Christmastide be your time for festive eating, for baked goods, candies, and once-a-year delicacies. Let any overindulgence be limited to that part of the holiday season intended for feasting and for feelings of being overjoyed!

7 ★ Enjoy a Quiet Day—A Fast for the Soul

O renew us, Lord, we pray,
With thy Spirit day by day,
That we ever one may be
With the Father and with thee.
—Wordsworth

A fast for the soul often takes the form of a Quiet Day: *a day away, a day of retreat, a day of abstinence from the world.* You owe it to yourself to enjoy the benefits of a Quiet Day, sometimes referred to as a Day of Silence or a Day of Contemplation.

A number of churches or dioceses sponsor such days during Advent. Monasteries specialize in them. Many retreat houses, campgrounds, and facilities operated by religious orders offer facilities for Quiet Days during Advent. Call around. Plan ahead. Anticipate a day of peace, and a new experience. Even though you may not be a member of the denomination sponsoring the Quiet Day, you generally will be welcome to participate without any type of coercion or questioning.

Some organized quiet days have more structure than others; some even have speakers or designated leaders who help focus group times of devotional reflection or prayer. Look for an opportunity that offers you minimal involvement with others. A Quiet Day is a fast, of sorts, from other people.

Create Your Own Quiet Day   Although it takes more discipline and effort, you can also create your own Quiet Day. The elements of a Quiet Day are fairly common from group to group, and from person to person.

- *Establish quiet.* No television. No radio. No conversations. No music. The most purely defined Quiet Day is a day of fasting for the ears, a day without noise or input of any kind. Do not even talk to yourself, and offer only limited vocalized prayer.

- *Establish solitude.* This is your day to be alone. It is not a family day or even a day to share with friends or spouse.

- *Establish rest.* This is not the day to clean the house, run five miles, or finish a craft project. A Quiet Day is a day of rest for your body.

- *Establish contemplation.* A Quiet Day is a day for the soul. It is a day intended for fasting *from* the world with the purpose of spending time *with* the Lord. It is not simply a day of turning off the noise, activity, and routine of the world. It is a day for turning *from* the world *to* heaven.

Listen to the Lord   Spend your Quiet Day as if you were inhabiting an outer court of heaven itself, listening to the wisdom of the Lord. Read His Word. Indulge in the opportunity to spend hour after hour reading Scripture. Let the verses of the Bible soak into your soul. You may want to have a pen and notebook handy for recording any inspirations or special insights you experience.

And finally, strive to take a little of that "quiet" you

encounter back into your regular routine of living. You may find that you want to turn off the television set during Advent. You may want to limit what is played on the family stereo.

Make Advent a time for a mental and spiritual fast. Separate yourself from the normalcy of your routines and surroundings and set yourself apart to be in His presence.

8 ★ Keep an Advent Prayer Book

Pour light upon us from above
And fire our hearts with ardent love.
—Latin Hymn

As you contemplate the mysteries of the Lord and enjoy quiet times of prayer during the Advent season, record your prayers. Write them down. Create your own Advent prayer book.

Len, a personal acquaintance, has a book in which he has written a prayer for each of the last six Christmas seasons. His prayer for each year is one, long, continuous statement. He adds a phrase, a paragraph, or an entire page every few days during Advent. During the twelve days of Christmas his prayer shifts into praise; the entries read as a great outpouring of spontaneous and free-flowing adoration of the Lord. The final segment of his prayer, an Epiphany prayer of sorts, is a simple expression of thanksgiving for Jesus and for the gift of language with which to pray. One year, Len's Christmas season prayer was twenty-six pages long; another year, it was only ten pages.

Christmas Blessing Book Darlene and Bob have a Christmas prayer book of a different sort. They invite the guests who come to their home during the holiday season, relatives as well as friends, to write a blessing for them and for their family in their "Christmas Blessing Book." Each person uses a new page of the book. Then, on Christmas afternoon, Darlene and Bob sit down with the book and, at the bottom of each page, add their own prayers for each relative or friend.

"We pray in a very concrete way for each one," says Darlene. "Some years we write in full paragraphs; other years we've just put a few key words under each friend's name. But, our prayers are always for specific needs and blessings that we want to see happen in the person's life.

Personal Prayer Book   Ginger has yet another type of prayer book that she keeps for the holiday season. She writes a short prayer for each day of Advent and then, since she is an artist, she illuminates the prayers with scenes directly related to her holiday celebrations. After a lovely evening with friends at a candlelit chamber concert, she wrote:

> Out of the darkness, light. And for the darkness of the soul, music. Surely that is what the angels had in mind as they sang for the shepherds watching their flocks near Bethlehem.

To accompany her prayer, she sketched a border of musical notes that took on the appearance of angels in flight. A lovely prayer—in both word and image! Ginger's prayer book is a work of art that will long be cherished by her children.

- Prayer prepares the heart.

- Prayer kindles the fire of Christmas love.

- Prayer gives expression to the deep recesses of the soul.

- Prayer is at the heart of Advent.

9 ★ Plan Your Holiday Season

Our hope and expectation,
O Jesus, now appear.
—Rejoice, Rejoice, Believers

Don't let Christmas catch you by surprise. Plan for it. In the fall of the year, and no later than the first of December, have a family meeting in which you sit down to make plans for the entire holiday season.

- *Mark your calendar.*

- *Make your lists.*

- *Allocate responsibilities.*

- *Make sure that everyone knows when and where and what and who.*

- *Post your lists and calendar in a prominent, easy-to-read place in your home.*

- *And then, relax and enjoy the plans you have made.*

Important Dates   Your plans for the holiday season will, of course, depend on your own unique family structure and traditions. To get you started on your Christmas season calendar, here are some important dates to remember.

- If you are planning to host a party, backtrack on your calendar and record the dates that the invitations need to be mailed, the prebaked items prepared for the freezer, and the buffet centerpiece ordered from the florist.

- Put down the dates recommended by the U.S. Postal Service for mailing overseas parcels, domestic parcels, and greeting cards.

- Set aside times for shopping. Make a list of any items of clothing that you may need to purchase for special parties, performances, or trips. Allow extra time for unexpected weather delays and for unsuccessful shopping trips. Give yourself a "second shot" at finding the right gift, the right item of apparel.

- Be sure to put down the date of your child's Christmas pageant or school concert.

- Decide which day you are going to purchase your Christmas tree, and set aside a time to put it up. Decide when you are going to put up your other household decorations.

- You may want to set aside a day for baking, another day or evening for writing Christmas cards.

Family Projects Make a list of things for your children to do. Give them specific projects for the holiday season. Prepare a craft box of scissors, glue, and paper, and keep it readily available for their use.

Share the responsibilities for decorating, shopping, and cooking. Make a schedule; pass out assignments.

Set aside several family nights for sharing from your Advent journals, singing carols, reading a Christmas book, sharing the Christmas story. You might even set aside a couple of "mystery" nights, times that are unplanned as to event but planned as to your togetherness.

By planning in this way, you'll quickly notice conflicts and thus avoid last minute scurrying or tearful disappointments. You may also discover that you are planning too much into too few days. Eliminate some of the activity! Avoid the tension of make-or-break deadlines and killer agendas.

Very often, it is those who don't plan who find themselves in such a whirl of disarray that they can't truly enjoy any one aspect of the season. Baking is no fun because they forgot to purchase baking powder. Decorating is no fun because they can't find an extension cord.

Keep your schedule streamlined. Arrive at Christmas ready for celebration, not exhausted from preparation. Don't be tripped up by unwanted surprises that occur as the result of details overlooked or events unremembered. Let the foremost surprise of Christmas be one that the Lord brings into your heart!

10 ★ Participate in a *Messiah* Sing

No vision ever brought,
No ear hath ever caught
*   Such rejoicing;*
We raise the song, We swell the throng,
To praise thee ages all along.
—Nicolai

One of the most memorable evenings I have ever spent during a holiday season was my participation in a *Messiah* Sing.

In accepting the invitation of friends (who *can* sing well), I dutifully purchased Handel's *Messiah* choral book along with my ticket to the evening of music making, rehearsed the alto lines, made a silent vow to lip-sync as well as anyone ever had, and determined that I would enjoy the evening.

The gothic cathedral, with simple wreaths and garlands hung tastefully on its paneled walls, was truly beautiful that evening. The organ was magnificent. The audience was attired in styles ranging from satins and silks to tweeds and turtlenecks.

I had anticipated a magnificent musical experience, something akin to being enveloped in surround-a-sound choral splendor. What I had not anticipated was the holiness of a divine appointment.

The lyrics to the *Messiah* are drawn from Scripture, and as the words of the prophets rolled over me and swirled around me, I had a new understanding of Advent, a stark and abrupt realization that this beloved, tender, adorable baby had, indeed, been born to die.

> Surely He has borne our griefs and carried our sorrows.
> He was bruised for our transgressions;
> He was wounded for our iniquities.
> The chastisement of our peace was upon him.

Somehow in the midst of drive-by nativity scenes and "Frosty the Snowman," we tend to miss that fact. Here was a child born with the sole purpose of being God's sacrifice for human sin. This infant in the manger is not just another cuddly baby over which to coo. He is a Lamb marked for death, on your account, on my account.

By the end of the evening, I had abandoned lip-syncing. I readily admit that my tears flowed freely. I joined in with the triumphant audience as we rose to our feet and sang at the top of our lungs:

> And He shall reign forever and ever.
> King of kings, and Lord of lords.
> Forever and ever,
> Hallelujah, hallelujah. Hallelujah!

Someplace during your Advent journey to Christmas, I invite you to experience Handel's *Messiah*. Most cities have at least one church or choral group that sponsors such a group singing of this oratorio. If not, settle yourself down for an evening with this music in your own home. Turn up the volume. Let the words and music billow through your soul.

> Who is the King of glory?
> The Lord strong and mighty.
> He is the King of glory!
> But first, death on a cruel and bloody Cross.

The first and second Advents, and our personal advent, converge at that point.

11 ★ Attend a Lessons and Carols Service

Grant us grace to see thee, Lord,
Mirrored in thy holy word;
May we imitate thee now,
And be pure, as pure art thou.
—Wordsworth

Many Catholic and traditional Protestant churches have a Lessons and Carols service during Advent. If you have never attended such a service, avail yourself of the opportunity.

The service is a sequence of readings from the Old Testament interspersed with the singing of traditional hymns that foretell the birth of Jesus. Christians of all persuasions are likely to feel at home in this service.

You can also have your own private Lessons and Carols service with your family or a group of friends. Or, you may want to plan a Lessons and Carols service as part of a Sunday school class, prayer group, or fellowship group.

Prepare Your Own Service *First, make a list of Scriptures that you want to read.* Focus on the prophetic words about the Messiah. You may want to include several or all of the following passages:

Genesis 3:14–15	Isaiah 7:13–14
Genesis 22:18	Isaiah 9:7
2 Samuel 7:12–17	Isaiah 11:1–9
Psalm 89:3–4	Isaiah 42:1–7
Job 19:25	Isaiah 52:13–53:12

Isaiah 55:3–4   Zechariah 9:9–10
Jeremiah 23:5–6   Malachi 3:1–2
Ezekiel 34:23   Luke 1:26–35
Micah 5:2–3

If you are planning this as a group activity, you may want to write out the passages beforehand, or have them clearly marked in a large print Bible that you will use during the service.

Second, choose what you want to sing. Some common hymns are:

"Come Thou Long-Expected Jesus"
"O Come, O Come, Emmanuel"
"Lo! He Comes with Clouds Descending"
"O Come, All Ye Faithful"
"O Little Town of Bethlehem"

You don't need to be limited, however, to a traditional hymn. You can choose any hymn that points toward the lordship of Jesus Christ and His rule and reign as Messiah. As closely as you can, match the hymns to the lessons you plan to read.

Third, consider opening and closing the service with prayer. You may also want to leave times for prayer between sets of lessons and carols. The prayers need not be long. You may want to write out simple sentence prayers that can be used to introduce a period of silent prayer. For example, after singing "O Come All Ye Faithful," a member of the group may pray, "Lord, help us to be faithful, joyful, and triumphant as we come to behold you as Christ the Lord."

A Lessons and Carols service compels us to recall that Jesus was the most expected baby ever to be born.

12 ★ Set Aside a Daily Prayer Time

Light and life to all he brings,
Risen with healing in his wings.
                    —Hark! the Herald Angels Sing

Make the weeks before Christmas a concentrated time for prayer. Make a *commitment* of your time and love to pray.

- *Pray daily.* Don't allow yourself to get so caught up in festivities and the "doing" of Christmas activities that you neglect the One who made the season possible.

- *Pray with an attitude of thanksgiving.* Find something every day for which you can give thanks. Think back over the last year. For what are you thankful? In what do you feel blessed?

- *Pray that the Lord may heal you and make you whole during this season.* Ask Him to help you keep your priorities straight, your mind fixed on him, your expressions of love to be genuine.

- *Pray for those you love.* Pray that their needs will be met, their hearts comforted, their lives filled with the good things of God.

- *Pray for those who do not know the Lord,* those who

have not heard of His coming. Pray for those who
are not expecting His return.

- *Pray for the peace of Jerusalem and for peace among
  nations.* Pray for the Christians who are under per-
  secution around the world, that they may experience
  His coming to them in the hour of their trial.

- *Pray for those in your parish or congregation who are
  in need.* Remember those who are lonely, sick,
  homeless, unemployed, bereaved, or in the hospital
  during the holiday season.

- *Pray for those who lead your church.* Call out the
  names of your pastors and their family members.

- *Pray that Jesus may be born anew in the manger of
  your heart.*

- Praise the Lord that the Scriptures promise that He
  will both hear and answer you when you pray.

Prayer holds our focus on the fact that Jesus came to
dwell among us, that by Him, and in Him, and through
Him—to the glory of the Father—all honor is due, now
and forever. He is the One who has come to us. Let us
make Advent a time for coming to Him.

13 ★ Ask Forgiveness of Those You Have Wronged

All glory be to God on high,
And to the earth be peace;
Good will henceforth from heaven to men
Begin and never cease!
　　—While Shepherds Watched
　　Their Flocks by Night

One of the foremost words associated with the holiday season is *peace.*

- *Peace on earth.*

- *Peace—goodwill to men.*

- *Peace among brothers.*

- *Peace in our hearts.*

True peace, however, comes only as the result of forgiveness.

Make Advent your season to ask forgiveness of those you have wronged during the past year. Don't arrive at the Christmas manger bearing a burden of guilt, hate, vengefulness, or bitterness.

Seek to Make Amends　Go to those you have hurt. Express your heartfelt regret. Seek to make amends. Ask for their forgiveness. Do you feel as if you are the one who has been wronged? Go to the other person and ask his or her forgiveness anyway. You may well find yourself being asked for forgiveness in return.

Have you hurt someone or been hurt by someone who is no longer alive or with whom you no longer have contact? Release them to the love of the Lord.

Let Go of Your Pain   Make Advent the season when you let go of the memories of your pains, sins, and regrets. My friend Clarissa does this in a tangible fashion. She purchases one black candle at the beginning of Advent and places it in a small crystal candlestick.

Each night during her prayer time, Clarissa lights this black candle as she asks the Lord to bring to her remembrance those things for which she needs to repent. She also asks the Lord to heal her of hurt feelings and to free her from resentments that she has been harboring in her heart. "I allow these things to go up in smoke. I refuse to remember them or to cling to them after that night." According to Clarissa, "Christmas appears a lot brighter when I don't have to view it through the soot of my own sin!"

14 ★ Help Decorate a Jesse Tree

For want of clothing they did him lay
All in a manger, among the hay.
—The First Nowell

Does your church or civic group have a Jesse Tree? If not, you may want to suggest the tradition. Or, you may want to have a small tree in your own home that you designate as a Jesse Tree.

A Jesse Tree is decorated with ornaments associated with Old Testament events, from creation to the birth of Jesus. The tree's name comes from the prophecy about Jesus in Isaiah: *"A shoot will come up from the stump of Jesse; from his roots a Branch will bear fruit"* (Isa. 11:1 NIV).

Invite your children (or your Sunday school class) to make ornaments for the tree. They can be made from construction paper or by cutting out magazine pictures and gluing them to lightweight cardboard. Punch a hole in the top of each ornament and tie a string through it so you can hang it.

Symbolic Ornaments Ornaments might include such items as a rainbow (Noah's ark), a scroll of paper (the Law), a star, a flame (Moses' burning bush), an apple (Garden of Eden), a photograph of a lamp (the word of God being a "a light on our path"), a postcard of a river scene (the Jordan River), a brightly colored piece of paper (Joseph's coat), a crown (the kings of the Old Testament), and so forth.

Encourage your children to look up the passages of Scripture that relate to the ornaments they make and to read those passages aloud. As a whole, a Jesse Tree visually tells the story of Jesus' heritage. It also stands as a symbol that Jesus is the true "tree of everlasting life" in our lives today.

Items of Warm Clothing

In many churches, a Jesse Tree is used to collect items of warmth for the poor or homeless. The tree is decorated with hats, scarves, gloves, mittens, socks—virtually any small item of warm clothing. In this way, the Jesse Tree becomes a reminder that just as Jesus was a Branch of Jesse bearing fruit in our lives, so we are to bear fruit in our world today, giving to others in need, just as He came to us in our need.

A Jesse Tree is a wonderful reminder that we have a rich and glorious heritage in Christ Jesus, a heritage firmly rooted in giving. We, too, are branches, even as He is the vine!

15 ★ Limit the Wish List

And we, too, may seek his cradle;
There our hearts' best treasures bring;
Love, and faith, and true devotion
For our Saviour, God, and King.
—Tours

Disappointment generally arises when we have expected more than we have received. Don't let Christmas be a time of disappointment. Expect only what you have been promised:

- *forgiveness for sins repented;*

- *healing for the brokenness of our lives;*

- *grace abundant and mercy unmerited;*

- *our needs to be met in His sufficiency;*

- *joy out of sorrow and gladness out of mourning;*

- *answers to prayer; and*

- *desires of our heart to be fulfilled when we act in faith according to heaven's will.*

His promises are too numerous to recount. His blessings are too wonderful to contain. It is His miracle that we must await with a spirit of expectation. Look to the Lord for your gifts this Christmas season, and you won't be disappointed.

"But what about my children?" you say. Encourage your children to rethink their wish lists.

Set Limits on Wish Lists   You may want to set limits on your children's wish lists:

- limit the amount of money that items cost;

- limit the types of items that can be included—for example, only two toys, at least one item of clothing; and

- limit the items that are for their personal use. You may want to encourage your child to think of one item on their wish list that they would like to see given on their behalf to someone else.

Encourage Giving Lists   Always balance wish lists with giving lists. When your child says, "I want . . ." ask your child, "What do you want to *give?*" Involve your child in choosing presents for others. Let him use his allowance money for that purpose (or, at least, part of his allowance to help with part of the purchase). Encourage your child to make gifts and to be creative in her gift giving.

Above all, ask your child what he would like to receive from Jesus this year, and what he wants to give to Jesus. Give examples by letting him hear your own wish-and-giving petitions.

Discuss with your child the real gifts that Jesus came to give. Assure your child that those are gifts that Jesus not only wants to give but is eager to give and that those are the true gifts to expect not only at Christmas, but all through life.

16 ★ Reflect on His Coming

Word of the Father,
Now in flesh appearing:
O come let us adore him.
—O Come, All Ye Faithful

What difference does it make that Jesus came? That is a question worth pondering throughout the Advent season.

What would our world be like if He hadn't been born? Would we still be awaiting His birth? Would we be hopeful that He might come in our lifetime? On what would we base our faith? In what ways would our faith be different?

How would we feel if He hadn't promised to send us another Comforter when He returned to Heaven? Why is it important to us that He said He would return?

Advent is a good time for family discussions on these and other questions. Ask "what if?" questions. Put yourselves in the shoes of those who lived five years before Jesus was born.

Think About the Incarnation   In your own private devotional times, you may want to make a list of "reasons I'm glad Jesus came to the earth." That's what Cynthia did one Christmas season. She recently told me about her experience.

"Each day of Advent, I wrote in my personal journal just one reason I was glad that Jesus had been born, and then I stopped to reflect on that reason several times during the day—as I rode the subway into work, as I walked to my office, and so forth.

"All day I thought about what I had written. I couldn't seem to get away from that one thought for an entire week, as I pondered all that *Savior* means—healer, deliverer, redeemer.

"Gradually I explored other avenues of thought: 'I'm glad He came so I have someone to call Lord'; 'I'm glad He came so I can know what God is like'; 'I'm glad He came so I can have an abiding sense of joy in my life.' "

You may want to suggest that your Sunday school class, Bible study group, or fellowship group reflects on His coming in the way that Cynthia did. Start with a list of words that convey concepts of utmost importance to you: Salvation, forgiveness, freedom, joy, love, fellowship, security, friendship. Then reflect on the way Jesus indwells these concepts in your life.

Encourage your children to make a list of reasons they are glad that Jesus came to the earth. My young friend Catherine, age eight, wrote in her Advent scrapbook, "I'm glad Jesus came so we could have a Christmas tree. I like Christmas trees. I like the colored lights on our tree and the way the tinsel shows the colors of the lights. That's like us. Jesus is like the lights on the tree. We are like the tinsel that gets to reflect the light."

17 ★ Experience a New Worship Tradition

*Pray you, dutifully prime
your matin chime, ye ringers;
May you beautifully rime
Your eve-time song, ye singers.*
—Ding Dong! Merrily on High

During the Advent season, experience Christmas through the eyes of a different denomination or different branch of the Church. You may be amazed and delighted at what you see.

Christmas, as no other holiday, unites Christians. Believers around the world celebrate Christmas. Its celebration cuts across all cultures, all ages, all nationalities. The message of Christmas is one to which all Christians adhere. "Born of a virgin" is a line that appears in every well-known creed.

Try a Variety of Experiences Christmas services provide a wonderful opportunity for teaching your children that Christians are "mostly alike and only a little bit different" in their beliefs.

At Christmas, you will probably feel at home in just about any church you enter. Try it and see for yourself.

- Midnight Mass. If you have never been to one, be prepared for incense, candles, Holy Communion, music—and "feeling" the arrival of Christmas in a way that you may never have felt it before.

- Christmas cantata. This service is common to many evangelical churches. Newspaper ads will tell you what musical is being performed in which church and when. This is a season for pageantry, a time when costumes and scenery fill bare platforms. Your children won't be bored; they may well be in awe! Don't be shy about singing or applauding.

- Choir concert. A local college chorale may be presenting a concert in a local cathedral.

- "Living Christmas Tree" presentation. Your children will be delighted at the organization of choir members into a giant tiered "tree."

- Outdoor, drive-by Nativity program. Live animals and actors portray the scenes most commonly associated with the birth of Christ. Christmas will seem more real to your children after they have seen real sheep, real donkeys, and maybe even a real camel or two!

- Walking tour of downtown churches. Take a tour on your lunch hour, enjoying the variety of decorations used by various churches and picking up a few tips for your own use, too.

- Bell-ringing service.

- Madrigal feast. This features a festive banquet, ye olde caroles of yore, and elaborate costuming.

- Evensong concert. You will enjoy a concert featuring the local boys' choir during the Advent season.

Look for new opportunities to welcome the birth of the Christ child.

18 ★ Enjoy the Small Moments

The tree of life my soul hath seen,
Laden with fruit and always green:
The trees of nature fruitless be
Compared with Christ the apple tree.
　　　　　　—Jesus Christ the Apple Tree

Advent is a good time to make a decision to enjoy the "small moments." Pick them from the myriad of dazzling impressions and savor them, as apples plucked from a heavily laden apple tree.

"But, how can I decide that?" you may ask. Just do. Say to yourself, "I *will* find beauty and pleasure in many small things this season. I will savor each moment as special. I will gather memories as the ripe fruit of this season. I will choose to receive what God and others give."

Become Attuned in a New Way Capturing the little moments requires only that you choose to activate your senses and become attuned in a new way to what may have become ordinary.

- *Choose to smell Christmas.* Crush a small twig of evergreen in your hand. Stop to stir up the potpourri at least once a day. Stick cloves in oranges and scatter them throughout the house. Simmer a blend of holiday spices in boiling water on your kitchen stove to fill your house with a holiday aroma.

- *Choose to see Christmas with new eyes.* Stop to stare.

Don't whiz by the elaborately decorated Christmas tree at the store's mall entrance. Pause for a moment to enjoy its beauty, to take in the design and color and texture. Take time to watch the icicles melt from the edge of your roof or to watch the ice webs form on your windowpanes.

- *Choose to hear Christmas in a new way.* Listen for the sound of those Salvation Army bells. Kenneth always gives his two little girls, Carolyn and Cathy, two quarters before they go shopping, "one for each pocket." And then they "listen for the bells." The secret mission of each shopping trip is to find at least two bell ringers and to give each one a quarter. "Listening for the bells keeps their minds less focused on the abundance of toys in the store windows," says Ken. "And it gives them an opportunity to give at Christmas. All in all, the girls probably contribute only a total of ten dollars, but I think they have a sense that they are truly involved in the charity of the season. I hope that their giving will become a lifetime pattern."

- *Choose to enjoy the many textures of the season*—the slippery wrapping paper, the embossed greeting card, the satiny ribbons, the velvet skirt, the taffeta dress, the fur-trimmed coat, the wooly mittens, the mohair sweater.

- *Choose to taste Christmas in small morsels.* Choose just one bite of everything from the buffet table. Savor each bite fully. Try a new flavor of tea or coffee. Give yourself five minutes to nibble a cookie.

Make Christmas a sensory sampler. Gather its small moments and weave them together to create your own holiday tapestry of sights and sounds and smells and tastes and sensations.

19 ★ Say "I Love You" to Someone Who Hasn't Heard It in Awhile

News of great joy, news of great mirth,
News of our merciful King's birth
—On Christmas Night

The days before Christmas are a time when many of us pause to remember those we love with gifts, cards, phone calls, or quiet moments of recalling happy times together. Christmas is also a time we remember that God loved us so much that He sent His only Son so that we might come into a new and deeper relationship with Him. The message of Christmas is that of divine and human love outpoured.

"I Love You" Sometimes, in the showing of our love, we forget the telling. Find a moment this Advent season to tell someone that you love him or her in *words.* Say, "I love you" to someone who hasn't heard it in awhile.

- *To a parent* who hasn't heard from a runaway child —but also to a parent who sees her child every day. Don't assume that the other person knows of your love if you haven't said so recently.

- *To an aunt, uncle, or grandparent* who hasn't been contacted in awhile. Is there a relative that you haven't seen or called in awhile? Take the time for a holiday season visit.

- *To a child,* grandchild, niece, nephew, godchild, or young neighbor. Children never get tired of hearing the words, "I love you" or "I sure do like you."

- *To a spouse.* Create a special holiday memory for just the two of you.

"I Appreciate You"   Love may be too strong an emotion for many other relationships you have. Still, Christmas is a good time to say "I appreciate you" or "I value you" or "I'm glad you are a part of my life."

Tell it to coworkers, bosses or employees, pastors and Sunday school teachers, the mail carrier, your child's bus driver, the next-door neighbors, the clerk who always gives you special attention.

Love is the "news of great joy, news of great mirth" that we sing about. In order for it to be news, it needs to be told. Make Advent your season for spreading the word!

20 ★ Learn About the Festival of Lights

Inflame our hearts with love's sweet fire,
That love of thee be our desire.
—O Jesu, Sweet Child

The Jewish feast of Hanukkah falls at some time during Advent. As an adopted son or daughter of Abraham, you can benefit from learning about this Festival of Lights in your own home.

Hanukkah is an eight-day celebration for the Jews. It marks the liberation of the Temple by Judas Maccabaeus from the control of the wicked Antiochus Epiphanes, who had defiled the Temple by sacrificing hogs on the sacred altar. The liberation came on the twenty-fifth day of the Hebrew month of Kislev, the third anniversary of the defilement. (It's not a great leap to see why the Roman Christians chose the twenty-fifth day of their month, December, as a day for celebrating the Lord's birth.)

Eight-Day Celebration In preparing for the re-purification of the Temple, the Maccabean liberators discovered that only one day's worth of holy oil remained in the Temple. An eight-day supply was necessary for the consecration and purification ceremony. Nonetheless, he poured out that day's cruse of oil and kindled it. Miraculously, it burned brightly for the full eight days.

Hence, an eight-day celebration was instituted in which Jewish families gather to light a series of eight candles, one each evening until all are lit. They give gifts to one another at this time and add oily foods (such as deep-fried potato pancakes and donuts) to their festive meals.

How might you share the celebration of Hanukkah?

- You may choose to have a Hanukkah lampstand in your home and to light the candles each night just as the Jewish people do.

- You may choose to celebrate the last day of Hanukkah and to invite each member of your family, or gathered group of friends or coworkers, to light a candle and pray.

- You may want to devote the Sunday school session that falls during Hanukkah to a discussion of Hanukkah symbols, and perhaps provide donuts for your class.

Hanukkah is a time for deliverance and purification. It is a time for anticipating the miraculous. So is Advent.

CHRISTMAS

A Season for Celebration

21 ★ Keep a Manger Scene Central to Christmas

The first Noel, the angel did say,
Was to certain poor shepherds in fields as
*   they lay;*
In fields where they lay keeping their sheep,
On a cold winter's night that was so deep.
—The First Noel

Give a manger scene prominence among your Christmas decorations. Many lovely ones are now available in ceramic, wood, metal, glass, and porcelain. The one we had when I was a child was made of paper, very simple in design. It was always the first Christmas decoration to be displayed each year. Over the years, the sheep got a bit tattered, and a few tab *A*'s no longer fit easily into slot *B*'s. One of the palm trees disappeared. The rest of that manger scene is still with us, though, yellowing with age and rapidly approaching antique status. It is a cherished family possession.

Consider using a manger scene in a dramatic way to tell the story of Christmas to your children over a series of days or weeks. That's the way my friend Suzanne and her family used a creche.

- On the first Sunday of Advent, they put out only the stable itself.

- On the second Sunday, they added donkeys and cattle to the manger scene.

- On the third Sunday, they put out the shepherds and their sheep at some distance away from the stable (usually on a bookshelf across the room). They put Mary and Joseph in another location—usually on the coffee table.

- On the fourth Sunday, they moved Mary and Joseph closer to the stable. They placed the wise men in a distant location, usually in an adjacent room.

- On Christmas Eve, they brought Mary and Joseph into the stable, hung the star, and added the angels to the scene. After a late church service, they placed the baby Jesus into the manger. They brought the shepherds to the stable and placed them around the manger.

- Throughout the twelve days of Christmas, they inched the wise men and their camels closer and closer to the scene. They removed the shepherds, stable, and animals, leaving only Joseph, Mary, and Jesus. They timed the arrival of the wise men to worship the baby Jesus to occur on Epiphany.

If you choose to keep your creche "in motion" as an ongoing storytelling device, you may want to combine the movement of the various pieces with the lighting of the candles on your Advent wreath and perhaps the singing of carols. Light the appropriate candle for each Sunday and sing as your children move the manger-scene figures into position. This is a good family reinforcement activity for events that take place in church and Sunday school during Advent.

22 ★ Chop Your Own Christmas Tree

The sight of thee at Christmastide
Spreads hope and gladness far and wide.
O Christmas tree, O Christmas tree!
Thou tree most fair and lovely!
—O Christmas Tree

Think of the plethora of Christmas customs, and what is one of the first images that comes to mind? Think of the many ways in which we celebrate Christmas in our homes, and what seems to be a common denominator? A Christmas tree!

It is difficult to imagine Christmas without Christmas trees. Their appearance in individual homes, however, is a custom that has been pursued only for the past two to three centuries. Prior to that, Christians tended to have a Christmas tree in the sanctuary of their parish church, where the tree generally remained unadorned.

What Trees Symbolize   Why have a Christmas *tree* in the first place?

Cedar trees, especially, are a symbol throughout the Old Testament for the strength and glory of God's people. Christmas trees are nearly always *evergreen* trees, reflecting the concept of eternal life, the promise to all those who believe in the One born at Christmas as the definitive sacrifice for our sin. Early believers in Rome took the evergreen branches, popular with the Romans who celebrated the lengthening of the days after winter solstice, and used them as part of their own religious services. They saw new and deeper meaning in the fronds of evergreen: the flexibility and strength of the evergreen branches symbolized the work of the Holy Spirit in the lives of those who follow Jesus Christ, the sweet-smelling odor symbolized the sweet-smelling sacrifice of their prayers, and the berries of the trees symbolized the fruit of the Spirit in their lives.

Why Trees Are Decorated   Tradition holds that Christmas trees began to be decorated when Martin Luther noticed the way in which the stars of heaven seemed to rest upon the branches of the great evergreen trees in the Black Forest. He brought a small tree into his home and adorned it with tiny candles that were lit on Christmas Eve as a way of expressing to his family the dual symbolism of Christ as Light of the World and as Eternal Savior. Others were quick to want to share in this meaningful method of celebration. Christmas trees in the windows of believers became a way of witnessing about one's faith to the surrounding community.

One of the most meaningful ways to rekindle a sense of the symbolic is to join with family or friends and cut your own Christmas tree.

- Place your cut tree in water as soon as possible and keep it in water, adding water daily. That will keep your tree as fresh as possible for as long as possible.

- You may want to bring an evergreen tree into your home early in Advent and leave it undecorated until Christmas Eve. Enjoy its fresh smell.

Christmas trees are not only beautiful. They are sermons in disguise. Hear their message.

23 ★ Make Your Own Greeting Cards

Heaven sings alleluya,
Alleluya the earth replies.
—We Three Kings of Orient Are

Second only to the custom of the Christmas tree seems to be the custom of exchanging holiday greetings. These greetings often take the form of Christmas cards or letters.

Darlene and George send a Christmas poem to their friends each year. They don't care if the rhyme isn't perfect and neither do those of us who receive their greetings.

Writer Timothy and graphic artist Debra send a tabloid-style news sheet, complete with sensationalized headlines, to update their friends on family happenings.

You may not be a poet, writer, or artist, but you still can be creative with your greeting cards. Try purchasing blank cards, or even postcards, and compose your own greeting.

Are you in the habit of sending a family portrait? Try an action shot or a creative twist on the old theme. I recently received a card with a black and white family photo of the family on the cover. The photo was of the family members tied together with a string of popcorn and a long rope of tinsel. Each family member had bows stuck on his or her sweatshirt in a haphazard manner, with ornaments dangling from the mother and daughter's ears. The son had a twig of holly between his teeth. The inside caption was handwritten: "From our branch of the human family tree to yours . . . we wish you many holiday smiles!"

Ask Your Children to Create Christmas Greetings

- Ask your artistic child to draw or paint a Christmas scene, and then contact your local printshop about turning it into your own greeting card.

- Purchase construction paper and let your children create your cards for you. Give them a stack of old cards to cut up or a stack of current holiday catalogs from which they may cut holiday pictures. Or, let them color or paint the cover of the card. Then, write an original family greeting on the inside.

- Karen and her children recycle last year's Christmas cards by turning them into this year's Christmas postcards. Says Karen, "We found that nearly 90 percent of the cards we received had beautiful cover artwork and that the opposite surface of that photo or illustration had been left blank. I let the children cut off the greeting side of the cards, and then we use the blank backs of the cover art for postcard-style greetings. The postage is cheaper, the children and I have a fun holiday project that we can do together, and we have beautiful greeting cards essentially for free. We also feel that we are doing something to help the environment by recycling the cards."

- In addition to the cards they send to others, one family has each child prepare a card for Jesus as something of a combined birthday and Christmas card. These cards are placed on the mantel over their fireplace throughout the entire holiday season.

Find a festive way to display the cards you receive. Stick them in the louvers of doors or windows. String them as garlands over doorways or string them along stair railings. Have a large bowl filled with them on the coffee table.

24 ★ Host a Christmas Play

Of his love and mercy mild
Hear the Christmas story:
O that Mary's gentle Child
Might lead us up to glory!
—Unto Us Is Born a Son

Turn your home into a theater and stage a Christmas drama. It may be a children's play, an adult drama, or an event for the whole family.

Plan a Children's Party If you are planning a children's party, invite your child's friends to come over for a couple of afternoons of planning and rehearsing. Encourage the children to make up their own play and to write it down, to plan their own stage directions, to design their own props and construct them, and to create their own costumes. Ask them if they would like to include songs in their play. If so, decide which ones. Let the children create their own invitations to the play, and perhaps even create a program for the performance. Decide upon roles for each child to take and have a run-through rehearsal.

Help your child duplicate the words of their play so that each child will have his own script. You may want to do this between the first and second afternoon sessions. Your child may want to illustrate the cover of the playbook, or let each child illustrate his own playbook on a subsequent day. On the day of dress rehearsal, let the children help you bake or decorate cookies as party refreshments.

Then, invite the parents of the children to an evening at your home in which the children present their performance and serve the cookies that have been baked. Have everybody join together to sing a couple of carols. You will have created a Christmas memory that will last a lifetime.

Plan an Adult Christmas Drama   Your Christmas theater need not involve children, however. You may want an adults-only party for the reading of a Christmas play. Scout your local library for scripts of famous Christmas plays, or even work with your library to acquire a copy of a favorite movie script. (Start on this early in the fall!) Invite your friends over for a holiday party in which they are guaranteed to star. You may want to sit around casually and read the parts or enact them in true dramatic fashion. Have refreshments, of course, for a "cast party" after the performance!

Your party may be one just for your own family or extended family. What a great way to spend a wintry afternoon or evening, performing for one another in the context of family love.

Establish one overriding rule for all your holiday parties: *Applause only.* Set a festive tone in which no goof can be embarrassing and all performances are genuinely appreciated as a display of holiday joy.

25 ★ Throw a Birthday Party for the Baby Jesus

Son of God, of humble birth,
Beautiful the story;
Praise His Name in all the earth,
Hail the King of glory!
—Cook

Give a party in His honor! It may be a party for adults or for children . . . or for both. Think birthday party. After all, Christmas is one.

Bring Birthday Gifts Encourage the party guests to bring gifts of some type in honor of the baby Jesus. The gift may be

- *canned foods for the poor;*

- *articles of warm clothing for the homeless; or*

- *toys for needy children.*

One group of friends put together a complete Christmas tree for a needy family in their church. One brought the tree, another a string of lights, another colored balls, another tinsel, and so forth.

One large group, a Sunday school class of young couples and all their children, decorated a tree with one-dollar, five-dollar, ten-dollar, and twenty-dollar bills tied to ornaments to create a massive money tree for two missionary families who had been sent out from their church. They decorated their tree in the church social hall and had a group potluck as a birthday party for the baby Jesus.

A large card was prepared for each missionary family and was signed by all who came to the party. One person brought a Polaroid camera for recording the festivities so that the families in Nigeria and Brazil not only received the cash and card, but photos of their friends and of the decorated tree.

Another group got together for a "Christmas baking party in honor of our Savior's birth." One brought a sack of flour, another a sack of sugar, another a couple of pounds of butter, and so forth—all of the fixings for a massive batch of sugar cookies, which were decorated and then delivered in small brightly ribboned bundles to a shelter for homeless families in their community.

Deliver Gifts   If at all possible, make the central activity of your birthday party the delivery of gift items to their intended recipients. Bundle up the children and take them down to the Salvation Army to deliver the toys, or pay a visit to the children's ward at the local hospital to deliver the stuffed animals, or drive down to the food bank to deliver the canned goods.

Have a brief prayer time before you eat or before you leave to deliver gifts. Let everyone sing "Happy Birthday" to the babe laid in the manger.

26 ★ Have an Old-Fashioned Caroling Party

Then let us all most merry be,
And sing with cheerful voice-a,
For we have good occasion now
This time for to rejoice-a.
—God Bless the Master of This House

Make Christmas a time for sharing the gift of song.

- Invite your friends over for an afternoon or evening around the piano.

- Go to a retirement home, nursing home, or convalescent hospital with your church youth group, scout troop, or your own group of friends. Take along a guitar or sing a cappella.

- You may want to take a little cheer to your city or county jail, or join the services held for those at homeless shelters or crisis centers.

- In the mood for bundling up and caroling in the old-fashioned, door-to-door way? Consider calling on those in your parish who are homebound. Or serenade your local fire departments where men and women are on call twenty-four hours a day all through the holidays. You may want to honor your pastoral staff with a carolers' visit.

Provide a Sweet Morsel The original custom of caroling calls for those who are caroled to invite the carolers in for a hot beverage and a "sweet morsel." As a caroler, don't expect that. As one who is caroled, try to provide it. Keep a tin of cookies or candy aside for the sole pleasure of stop-by company. Put on the kettle, and enjoy a moment or two of fellowship. You may even be asked to join the caroling party.

Designate a Leader Indoors or outdoors, have one person designated as a group leader to begin and end the songs. Make sure you have plenty of copies of the words to the carols so that no more than two or three people need to share a songsheet. Choose carols both old and new. Sing verses familiar and unfamiliar.

And above all, sing with gusto. Keep the tempo bright and the mood upbeat. This is a time for rejoicing, and music is the language of joy!

27 ★ Make a Tape of Christmas Past

Long ago our fathers sang
Such a song on this same day.
—Patapan

Christmas is a time when extended families frequently have reunions or share meals. Make the most of those moments for audiotaping or videotaping your family heritage.

- Ask your family members to relate their favorite Christmas memories. Have them tell about their favorite surprise moments.

- Ask grandparents and other older relatives to recount tales of Christmases when they were children. Encourage your children to ask specific questions. *What kinds of gifts did you give at Christmas? What did you do at church to celebrate Christmas? Did you have football games on television during the Christmas season?*

- Explore differences. It may be difficult for children to imagine that parents or grandparents had different customs or climates. Children often don't know enough to ask questions that provoke interesting answers. Give them clues. *"Honey, did you realize that Grandpa grew up where it is very cold in the winter? Ask him about what did on snowy days. Ask him about caring for their animals during snowstorms."*

- If a visiting relative has experienced Christmas away

from home, or in time of war, or during the Great Depression, or in a hospital, ask about those Christmas seasons. What was different or special about those years?

- If your child's grandparents or other relatives emigrated to the United States from another country, ask about customs they enjoyed in the land of their birth.

- Are some of your in-laws from a different denomination? Ask about their holiday celebrations.

Keep It Casual   In some cases, your older relatives may be recorder shy. If so, you may want to have the recorder somewhat hidden and out of view (with the person's permission, of course) so that the person being interviewed won't be self-conscious. Keep the conversation casual. Allow for jokes and spontaneous responses from your children.

If you have a family songfest, carol sing, joke-telling hour, or variety show, or if you do your own Christmas program as a family, make a recording of that, too.

These memories on tape will become an increasingly valuable family treasure as the years go by. You may want to duplicate the tape and give a copy to each person present. As the years pass, your family will have a wonderful record of family events and customs.

28 ★ Build an Ornament Collection for Each Child

Let ev'ry house be bright;
Let praises never cease:
With mercies infinite
Our Christ hath brought us peace.
　　　　　　—Robbins

What makes a Christmas tree extra special? Ornaments! Ask any adult to recall for you the way in which her family Christmas tree was decorated during her childhood, and the likelihood is great that she'll be able to tell you in detail.

We had a green tree, generally four or five feet high, that we decorated with colored lights, brightly colored shiny balls (that broke fairly easily), and tinsel (that we were required to put on "unglopped"). The tree was topped by a big aluminum star that held the only white bulb in the string of lights.

A friend down the block always had a tall flocked tree with only blue ornaments hung on it. Another family's tree was flocked and covered with angel ornaments. Ah, those ornaments! They, in and of themselves, can become a tradition.

An Ornament a Year Consider buying a new ornament for each child each holiday season. Let the children open their own ornaments and add them to the tree on Christmas Eve. Keep each child's ornaments in a special box, clearly marked with his or her name. Box the ornaments for your child when he or she gets married, or send them to your child when he or she anticipates the first holiday season in his own apartment or home.

You may want to suggest an ornament collection to a godparent or an aunt or uncle as an ongoing Christmas gift. Your child will love the idea both now and later. Even small children enjoy pointing out their own personal ornaments on a family tree. The godparent or other relative will appreciate the opportunity to provide a gift that is reasonably priced and yet still meaningful.

When it comes time to decorate the family Christmas tree, let your child put his or her ornaments on the tree by himself and on the branch he chooses.

The ornaments you give to a child you love may have a theme:

- *wooden ornaments,*

- *angels,*

- *painted scenes on colored balls,*

- *silver-plated cutouts,*

- *handmade ornaments,*

- *antique ornaments,*

- *birds,*

- *bells.*

Then again, you may just want to choose what strikes your fancy in any given year.

Ornaments for All Occasions   You need not limit your collection to children. You may want to purchase an ornament each year of your marriage. Or exchange ornaments as adult friends, spouses, or relatives.

Keep a record of what ornaments have been given in which years and by whom. Store that list with the ornaments. You will appreciate having a master record as the years pass.

Christmas ornaments can be as meaningful as they are beautiful. Enjoy them! They are one of the loveliest ways to celebrate the season.

29 ★ Share an Old Tradition with a Child Who Has Never Experienced It

Bless all the dear children in thy tender care,
And fit us for heaven to live with thee there.
—Away in a Manger

There is nothing quite so wonderful as seeing the Christmas season through the eyes of a child. The bright lights. The gaily decorated presents with their eagerly anticipated secrets. The appearance of a glowing tree in the living room. The sound of bells from unfamiliar sources. To a child, so many things about Christmas are a first-time experience. What fun to share a child's wonderment. The adventure is this: seeing the old through a fresh pair of eyes.

Old Traditions

- A ride around town to see the lights.

- A slow walk past the animated figures in a department store display window.

- A performance of *The Nutcracker* ballet.

- A stage performance of Dicken's classic, *A Christmas Carol.*

- The turning on of several hundred thousand twinkling lights at a local outdoor shopping center.

- A last minute, Christmas Eve shopping trip to get that one last thing on the list.

- The renting of a favorite movie classic: *Miracle on 34th Street, It's a Wonderful Life, A Christmas Story.*

- A Christmas concert.

- A reenactment of a medieval Christmas feast.

New Traditions   Perhaps it is time to begin a *new* tradition. Do you feel there are no new ways to celebrate Christmas? Have you and your child "done it all"?

- What about a helicopter view of the city at Christmas to see the lights from a different vantage point?

- What about a noontime organ recital at the downtown cathedral?

- What about helping out with the senior citizen's "Christmas Ball"?

- What about volunteering to help deliver bags of food collected by a local charity?

Those are old Christmas customs for someone. Experience them as *new* Christmas season activities for yourself or your family.

And don't forget, the child you are exposing to an old Christmas tradition may even be yourself. If there is something you have always thought you would like to do or see at Christmas, make this the year to do it!

30 ★ See the Lights

Therefore, Christian men, be sure,
Wealth or rank possessing,
Ye who now will bless the poor,
Shall yourselves find blessing.
　　　　　　　—Good King Wenceslas

"Let's go to Panorama Drive," Mom would say one December Sunday night after church.

Craig and I would have our eyes peeled for the first house with a "major display," according to our private rating system. The ten-minute drive from our church up to the top of the bluff was filled with anticipation. And we were never disappointed.

The people who lived in the Panorama Heights area went all out. Nearly all had their houses outlined with lights, long before that became a universal custom across the suburbs of America. Nearly all of the houses had their front windows undraped so we could enjoy a drive-by glimpse of their beautifully decorated trees. (In those days, some were even flocked pink or baby blue. With silver ornaments and giant white angels, they were an awesome sight to an eight-year-old girl.)

Panorama Heights　Many of the homes had outdoor displays of some type. Cardboard cutouts of snowmen. Three-dimensional recreations of the manger scene. A giant, stuffed Santa Claus about to drop down the chimney.

We would drive by slowly, often in a long line of slow-moving cars, "oohing" and "aahing" our way from house to house, occasionally spotting a homeowner who would give a cheerful wave.

Christmas Tree Lane Second only to Panorama Drive was Christmas Tree Lane. About a mile of thirty-foot evergreens that graced the center divider of a major boulevard were decorated each Christmas with colored bulbs from tip to bottom branch. The avenue wasn't really called Christmas Tree Lane, that's just what it became every December. A slow drive up and down both sides of that spectacle was a fifteen-minute venture into wonderland.

The children in my life today look forward to seeing the homes around the pond off 31st Street, and the Children's Medical Center, and the white-light splendor of a local private school, and the old-fashioned, animated "display boxes" at the city's oldest shopping center. Their own tradition is in the making, and I have no doubt their imaginations are better for the experience each year of "seeing the Christmas sights."

31 ★ Read Aloud the Story

Now to the Lord sing praises,
All you within this place,
And with true love and brotherhood,
Each other now embrace.
—God Rest You Merry

There's no other story as wonderful. Stop to think about it. In what other story do we find an event more unsettling than that of an encounter between an angel and a virgin girl? A song more beautiful than that sung by Mary? A birth more mysterious and miraculous?

In what other story is there a scene more bittersweet than that of a baby born in an out-of-the-way stable? A moment more frightening and exhilarating than that of an angel interrupting the nighttime watch of shepherds? Or late-night quests more noble and furtive than those shepherds searching out a newborn baby in a town crowded with travelers?

In what other story do we have wise men traveling by camel to present exotic gifts to an unrecognized prince, or see major decisions made on the basis of dreams, or anticipate the urgency of a middle-of-the-night escape from the bloody sword of an hysterical king?

In what other story do we find a love more tender?

The Christmas story has it all. Take time this holiday season to read it again from start to finish.

- Read it aloud.

- Read it slowly.

- Read it with your family or by yourself.

- Read it from a different Bible translation from what you normally read or study.

Start with Luke 1:1 and when you get to Luke 1:56, go to Matthew 1:18 and read to Matthew 1:25. Return to Luke and read Luke 1:57 until Luke 2:38, and jump back to the entire chapter of Matthew 2.

No matter how many times you have read the story, you will gain a new insight—I guarantee it! That is the very nature of the Bible, to compel us to see something new about the Lord and our relationship to Him at each reading.

No story provides a wider range of emotions, a more important or intricately crafted plot, or a more interesting cast of characters.

Delight in the story. It is one that was written specifically for you.

32 ★ Try an International Christmas Custom

He rules the world with truth and grace,
And makes the nations prove
The glories of his righteousness
And wonders of his love.
　　　　　　—Joy to the World

What makes for a celebration is different for each one of us. Is it really any wonder that the happiest holiday of the year should find different expressions from culture to culture? This Christmas, try a custom from another country.

Belgium　　In Belgium, parades are common on Christmas Day. You can have your own parade, even if its just through the house. Let your children "dress up" in the wrapping paper, ribbons, and bows they have just taken from their gifts. In Belgium, the parades generally end at a church, where the people join in a special worship service. You can end your parade, too, with a time of prayer and thanksgiving to God that He has given you not only His son, but your own children.

Ireland　　In many Irish homes, candles are placed in every window of the house on Christmas Eve. This is intended to be a sign that Jesus is welcome in the house.

The candles are allowed to burn all night and tradition calls for them to be snuffed out only by a woman whose name is Mary. You may want to extinguish your candles after your children go to bed or use electric candles. (Be sure to keep such candles away from drapery or furniture.)

Poland   In Poland, some families do not eat at all during the day of December 24, but when the first star appears in the evening sky, supper is served. The meal is generally the most lavish and festive one of the entire year. A vacant chair is put at the table to send the message, "Jesus is welcome at our table." A peace wafer is given by the local priest or pastor to each family in his congregation, and at the Christmas Eve meal, this wafer is broken and shared with all those at the dining table as a symbol of mutual peace and good wishes.

Scandinavia   In Scandinavian countries, children traditionally put out grain on top of a long pole so that the birds can have their own feast on Christmas morning. Traps and fishnets are never put out on Christmas; legend holds that all of the animals in the world kneel and worship Jesus on that day. You may want to treat the birds in your neighborhood with a special wreath of seeds.

England   In some English homes, a giant yule log is placed in the hearth on Christmas Eve and while the log burns, carols and hymns are sung and plays are presented to tell the story of Jesus' birth. The custom calls for the children to be allowed to stay up until the log burns itself out, often late into the evening.

In exploring international Christmas customs, you will no doubt embark on an inner spiritual Christmas journey, too. Enjoy the trip.

33 ★ Look for the Christ Child in the Tragic Moment

Bring our ransomed souls at last
Where they need no star to guide,
Where no clouds thy glory hide.
—Dix

We would all like to be able to immunize the last six weeks of every year against any kind of sickness, accident, or tragedy. Unfortunately, we can't. Children get the mumps, cars slide into one another on the ice, surgeries are scheduled, and funerals are conducted during the holiday season. It doesn't seem fair, but it happens.

It may be helpful in those times to remember that the world was swallowed up in darkness and despair on the night that Jesus was first cradled in his mother's arms. Most of the world was living in a state of unredeemed tragedy, with very little joy and a great deal of fear, superstition, and wickedness on all sides.

Look for a Miracle The birth of Jesus into such a world was a definitive and magnificent move by the Almighty to penetrate all that is negative and destructive with the light of His all-powerful love. We can look for a similar miracle to happen for us when tragedy strikes. It has nothing to do with our natures or the nature of our tragedy; it has solely to do with His nature as Miracle Worker.

- A child becomes sick? Look for the opportunity to share Christmas books and puzzles that will help fill the hours.

- A friend becomes hospitalized? Look for the opportunity to have a conversation that runs deeper than normal everyday fare.

- A loved one dies? Look for the opportunity to give a hug and fix a meal.

Love extended during times of tragedy is exceedingly precious. Be a bearer of such love.

Is the tragedy happening in your own life? Try to approach the situation as an opportunity to grow, with a willingness to receive the help of others in the process. It may not be easy, I know, but look for God's grace extended, His love revealed. Receive every prayer, every kind word, and every tender touch as if it is coming directly from Lord Jesus.

Keep Your Perspective   Not all holiday difficulties, of course, are tragedies of such great magnitude. Some of them fall more into the genre of the absurd. The ice storm cuts all power to your neighborhood and plunges your home into darkness and your refrigerator into defrost. You forget to turn on the oven. The array of compact discs arrives as ordered, even as you receive word that the CD player itself is on back order. At such times, make up your mind to laugh. This, too, will make for memories. The memories will be sad ones only if you are.

At least once in your life, you will probably experience a holiday-season calamity or tragedy. Look for the Christ child in that experience. He has the capacity to turn a dingy stable into a royal courtroom. He has the desire to be the new star in your night sky.

34 ★ Invite a Foreign Student to Share Your Christmas Dinner

Those who never knew thee,
Those who've wandered far,
Lead them by the brightness
Of thy guiding star.
—Thring

Somewhere on a college campus is someone who will be away from family this Christmas. Your mission, should you choose to accept it, is to find this lonely soul and to welcome him or her into your home. If you do, you will have a Christmas you'll always remember. And, so will they.

Start looking for such a student in November, and extend your invitation early. That will give your guest the comfort of having something to which she can look forward during the grueling days of final exams. It will help him fight the twinge of homesickness he may feel as he watches others leave campus for holiday break.

Finding a Student How do you go about finding such a student? If your own child is in college, ask him if there's someone he would like to bring home for the holidays. If you don't have an on-campus contact, call the office of the dean of men, the dean of women, or the student activities director of a college or school in your area.

You may want to invite two or more students to your home rather than just one. Sometimes it's easier to get a conversation rolling if more than one student is present.

What kind of students are you likely to host? Most of the students who can't go home are foreign students. Be prepared for someone of a race and cultural background other than your own. Be prepared, too, for students who may come from different denominational or religious backgrounds. Other students have work obligations that keep them in town over the holidays. Still others are on tight budgets that preclude a midyear trip home.

Providing a Gift   Do you need to have a Christmas present for your guest? No. But, you certainly may provide a gift if you so desire. Choose something that is relatively neutral in nature.

Opening your home to a lonely student is a gift in itself. As one student wrote to his host home, "I can never repay you for having me in your home two years ago when I couldn't go home for the holidays, but I've decided to invite several students to my apartment for dinner *this* year. I thought you'd like to know that your act of kindness is being passed along."

Ask your guests about the Christmas customs of their families and their nations. Invite the students to help you in the kitchen and to help you with the cleaning up. (Chances are, they'll feel even more at home that way.) Invite them to stay for awhile after the meal to talk.

Christmas is a time for giving and receiving in unexpected ways. In this instance, you will no doubt receive far more than you give!

35 ★ Turn Your Thoughts to Praise

Alleluia, song of gladness,
Voice of joy that cannot die;
Alleluia is the anthem
Ever dear to choirs on high.
—Latin Hymn

Christmastide is not a time for your holiday meditation to end. It *is* a time for your periods of quiet reflection to turn to high praise. Make a list of those things that give you joy.

- Do you delight in children's laughter? Write it down.

- Do you relish secrets of surprises soon to be discovered? Make a note.

- Do tables set with festive china and linens give you pleasure? Add them to your list.

- Do you smile when you hear the cheerful calls of "Merry Christmas" as friends meet and part while shopping?

- Do you find deep fulfillment in the visits with friends you haven't talked to in awhile?

- Does the organ swelling to fill the cathedral on Christmas morning cause your own heart to swell? Praise the Lord!

A Praise Journal   Keep a journal of those wonderful moments that send your heart soaring and your mind turning to the goodness, greatness, and majesty of the Lord. Take time to thank Him for these, His gifts to you. Let your thanksgiving be generous, extravagant, unbridled. Let your appreciation for His gifts take on the same qualities as His outpouring of them.

The Lord delights in what gives you delight in the holiday season. He likes to hear that you appreciate His handiwork. He also likes to hear that you appreciate the work that He is in the cooperative process of creating through the lives of others—laughter, music, friendship, prayers, the works of human hands that point toward the glory of His presence.

He delights, too, in the pleasure you take in your own growth in Him. How much joy fills His heart when He sees that you see and value the wholeness and growth in your own life as you become more and more like His Son. After all, that's why He sent His Son to this earth . . . and to you.

36 ★ Read a Christmas Book as a Family

O Jesus, babe beloved! O Jesus, babe divine!
How mighty is thy wondrous love!
Fill thou this heart of mine
With that great love of thine!
—Traditional German Carol

Find a Christmas book of some length that you and your family can enjoy together during Christmastide. Choose a book that shares the Christmas message as it has been lived out during the nearly two thousand years since Christ's birth. Discover how writers have applied the meaning of His arrival on the earth to our lives.

Ask your librarian for help. A number of books have been written with a Christmas slant or a Christmas section. Several anthologies of Christmas short stories (both adult and children) are on the market.

Nearly all of these Christmas books are stories that tug at the heart and make one aware of God's love. In choosing a Christmas story to read as a family, set that as your foremost criteria. Let the librarian know you are in the market for a book that is part tear-jerker, part smile-causer, and above all, honoring to God.

Grace Livingston Hill, a Christian novelist whose works were published mostly during the first half of the twentieth century, wrote a number of short novels with a Christmas twist. The collected works of Pearl S. Buck and Charles Dickens include a number of Christmas selections.

Once you have settled on a book for the season, establish a procedure for your reading sessions.

If your children aren't yet readers, read to them. If they can read, let them read to you. Or, take turns.

- You may choose to read for a few minutes around the breakfast table after toast and before heading off to school or work.

- You may want to read together for a few minutes before or after dinner.

- You may want your reading time to fall between homework and bedtime.

Making the Story Exciting   Even teenagers enjoy hearing stories read, once they get used to the idea. Invite them to close their eyes and imagine the scenes, complete with background music and sound effects. Create your own family version of radio-drama days.

Keep some suspense going. Read only a few pages a day or a short chapter. Think in terms of a serial drama. Don't stop to discuss the story. Just read. Discussion can happen at other times during the day or after the entire book has been read.

A story read together during the holidays is really a gift from the family to the family. It is a gift that enriches the mind, blesses the soul, and establishes a foundation for family communication. How many other gifts can do so much?

37 ★ Toss Some Cones into a Roaring Fire

Take heart, for comfort, love, and hope
Come swiftly on the wing;
O rest beside the weary road,
And hear the angels sing.
—It Came upon the Midnight Clear

Pine cones are frequently woven into our holiday decorations, especially as a part of floral arrangements and wreaths. You can use pine cones in a variety of ways during the holiday season.

One April I found myself in the Sierra Nevada Mountains of California shortly after the great "mother pines" had shed their giant cones, many of them as long as twenty inches. I gathered as many as I could bundle into trash bags. In December of that year, I tied clusters of three giant cones together with holiday ribbons and gave them to friends as yule cones.

Pine cones are inexpensive items for craft projects, and they can be turned into delightful gifts when subjected to your creativity. My friend Roberta has made larger Christmas-tree-style centerpieces from pine cones, fashioned them into wreaths, and has spray painted very tiny ones as Christmas tree ornaments.

One of my favorite pine cone activities, however, is one with a spiritual dimension. It stems from an oral tradition that I encountered during that visit to the Sierra Nevada Mountains.

Letting Go of the Past Legend has it that mountain men used to gather on New Year's Eve and toss cones into their campfires as a way of letting go of the past year. This was a reflective time for them.

You see, a pine cone is really a seed pod. Its characteristic flares are the result of its having opened up to send tiny seeds into the forest. Those seeds feed forest animals and birds, and a certain number of them take root and replenish the forest. Once emptied of their fruit, the cones are often crushed under the weight of falling limbs, snow, and the feet of larger animals. Once crushed, they create a mulch that helps form the deep moisture-holding mat of the forest floor.

Burning the Cones Consider bringing a basket of pine cones to your hearth this year. Spend part of an evening with your family or friends tossing cones into your blazing fireplace. They make a beautiful, glowing sight as they burn. If you live in a place where fireplaces aren't common, create your own outdoor campfire, perhaps even at the beach.

- Let each person toss in one pine cone to stand for sin.

- Let one pine cone tossed into the flames stand for your mistakes, hurts and resentments, or the sorrows of the past year.

- Let one pine cone represent your hopes and resolutions for the coming year.

At the end of the evening, take a pine cone from the basket to carry with you to your office or kitchen desk, as a reminder all through the coming year of this prayer time and spiritual release.

EPIPHANY

A Season for Giving

38 ★ Celebrate Epiphany

That we like to thee may be
At thy great epiphany;
And may praise thee, ever blest,
God in man made manifest.
                                        —Wordsworth

Epiphany falls on January 6, the twelfth night of the twelve days of Christmastide. Indeed, Epiphany is sometimes called Twelfth Night.

"Manifestation"　　Epiphany literally means "manifestation" or "coming to light." It is the time set aside by the western Church for celebrating the Magi's heeding of the message they perceived in a brilliant star in the east. The event is regarded as the manifestation of Christ to the Gentile world. In Orthodox circles, the day is also used to commemorate:

- the baptism of Jesus (including the heavenly Father's *manifestation* of a descending dove on His beloved, chosen Son) as told in Luke 3:21–22;

- the presentation of Jesus in the Temple as an infant (a *manifestation* of the Messiah's birth to the Jews, represented by Simeon and Anna) as the story is told in Luke 2:22–38; and

- the transformation of water into wine at the wedding feast in Cana (the first miracle of Jesus and a *manifestation* of His supernatural power) as told in John 2:1–12.

Epiphany is an excellent day to turn your meditative thoughts to the manifestations of the Lord in your own life.

Epiphany is also a day for recalling the gifts that the wise men brought to Jesus, whom they regarded as a new king. They presented gold, a symbol of His kingship; frankincense, the incense that symbolized His priesthood; and myrrh, the expensive embalming ointment that symbolized His eventual death as a persecuted prophet.

Gift Giving on Epiphany

Epiphany is an ideal day for giving a special gift to someone you dearly cherish. Make your love manifest. In many Latin American countries, gifts are not exchanged *until* Epiphany. You may not feel comfortable doing that in your family, but you may want to hold back one gift for opening on Epiphany. It may be a gift of a spiritual nature—such as a new Bible, prayer book, hymnal, inspirational book or journal, or a piece of jewelry or art with religious symbolism.

You may want to make Epiphany your time for remembering the clergy in your church with a gift. Thank them for being "prophets, priests, and kings"—those who preach the word, pray for and minister to the people, and have spiritual authority—in your life and that of your local church.

Epiphany is also a good time for making a trip to visit someone you haven't seen in awhile. Bring tidings of great joy. Make your presence a gift to a friend or relative or homebound member of your church congregation.

Epiphany has many wonderful concrete and symbolic aspects to its celebration. Don't miss out by ending your holiday season too soon!

39 ★ Share Your Sweets

Nowell! Nowell! Nowell!
Nowell sing we loud!
God today hath poor folk raised
And cast a-down the proud.

The holiday season is associated with the wonderful aromas of baked goods. More than any other time of year, our culinary thoughts turn to cookies, candy, and baked delights. The traditional list of Christmas goodies is a long one, and virtually every family has its own favorites:

- yule-log cakes

- candy canes

- boxes of chocolates

- Christmas cookies

- gingerbread houses

- Christmas puddings

- fruit cakes

The aroma of baking also says "home" in a special way. Warmth. Family. The fun of cooking alongside someone you love. A hot cup of tea and the coziness of a kitchen chat. Mix and stir. All of these concepts blend well with our concept of Christmas celebrations.

And what of those who have no home or are far away

from home at Christmas? The holiday season is a time for sharing the products of our kitchens with them.

Plan a Baking Spree   Take one of those wintry, no-school vacation days or evenings between Christmas and New Year's, and embark on a cookie-baking spree. Make it a family activity or invite several friends to join you. Nobody is too young or too old to be part of the action. Even toddlers can lick spoons, and Grandpa can usually be coaxed to crack pecans. Let the children help blob the dough onto the baking sheets and decorate the sugar cookies. Allow for nibbling along the way!

As various batches of cookies cool thoroughly, begin to count out an assortment of them into small plastic bags. Call in advance to see how many cookies per bag will be appropriate—a dozen and a half per family, six in an individual baggie? Tie the bags with pretty Christmas ribbons, and then head for the homeless shelter.

No time or money for that much baking? Do you receive an abundance of candy from clients, business associates, or vendors during the holiday season? Share your abundance!

Start a "Cookie Pool"   Perhaps your entire office staff would like to have a "cookie pool," each person bringing three or four dozen cookies of the same type (which takes less time for each baker). Then take a lunch break to mix an assortment of cookies into baggies.

In addition to sharing your gifts with homeless persons, you might also remember our servicemen and women who are on overseas assignments. Cookies baked during the Christmas season will be even more welcome upon their arrival a few weeks later when hardly anyone else has thought to send sweets. Ask your local military recruitment offices for suggestions as to the types of cookies and candy that travel well, and how best to package your items for an uncrumbled arrival.

Put yourself into the shoes of a homeless person or one who is far away from home at Christmas. What would you like to receive as a small gift of culinary love from an unknown source at Christmas? What flavors or treats would you miss the most if you were suddenly without your kitchen? Give what you would most like to receive.

40 ★ Buy Your Gifts Early

All our costliest treasures bring,
Christ, to thee our heavenly King.
—As with Gladness Men of Old

One of the most frequent resolutions I hear shortly after Christmas is this: *"Next year I'm not going to be so busy during the holiday season."*

Much of the hustle and bustle of the Christmas season seems to involve shopping. While it is fun to wade into the crowds periodically, shopping night after night or day after day can be wearying and can detract from the holiness of the season.

Try a simple twofold rule of thumb: buy or make all your gifts before Advent and give gifts as late as Epiphany (January 6).

This will accomplish several goals:

- *First, it allows you to spend more time throughout the year thinking about people and planning gifts for them.*

Shop sales. Pick up gifts as you take your summer vacation. Get items as you see them. We've probably all had the experience of seeing an item and saying, "That looks just like so-and-so." Act on those impulses.

- *Second, planning in advance allows you to make gifts.*

Crafted items may not be all that less expensive, but they certainly are an opportunity to reflect your creativity, your talent, and to incorporate the gift of your time into a present.

Be sure to allow yourself enough time for a hand-crafted project.

- *Third, planning in advance allows you to spread out the financial expense of gift-giving.*

Spending $25 a month for ten months is a lot easier than coming up with $250 in a matter of days. Set a goal of purchasing at least one or two gifts a month.

- *Fourth, planning in advance allows you to shop through catalogs, sometimes at a discount.*

You can often find unusual items available through holiday catalogs, many of which start arriving in the first weeks of September. Make your decisions and purchases early.

- *Fifth, advance planning allows you the luxury of giving the unusual and unexpected.*

Are you planning an outing to the zoo with your neighbor and her children? Be sure to take plenty of snapshots of her child, too. Then frame a couple of those as Christmas presents. Do you have a favorite photo from your summer vacation? Turn it into a poster.

As you collect gifts throughout the year, keep them in a locked trunk or a chest of drawers devoted to that purpose.

Avoid the tendency to rethink your purchases later.

Don't be pressured into spending more or purchasing additional gifts as Christmas draws nearer.

Taking the hustle out of shopping frees up time for Advent and Christmas experiences. Devote your holidays to doing, feeling, and just "being"—not shopping.

41 ★ Wrap an Extra Gift or Two

Since all he comes to succor,
By all be he adored,
The infant born in Bethl'hem,
The Saviour and the Lord.
—Traditional German Carol

Nearly all of us have an unexpected Christmas guest at some time in our lives. It may be the cousin who comes along as a "surprise" when you were only anticipating Aunt Joe and Uncle Lou. It may be a friend who shows up for a Christmas afternoon chat while he is in town for a visit with his parents. It may be a friend of your child's who had moved away and is back in town for only a day.

Often, such guests bring gifts with them. Anticipate that possibility! During the course of the year, purchase a few extra gifts. You might want to have at least two adult gifts, generic to both men and women, and at least one child's gift (that would span several ages).

Gift Ideas Here are some suggested gifts to have on hand.

- *Books,* especially those that are beautifully illus-trated or tell a classic story, are popular and versa-tile gifts. Blank books for journaling are appropriate gifts to have on hand for any adult (from teenager upward).

- *A selection of coffees or teas* in a sealed tin is an ap-propriate adult gift. You may want to buy several kinds of tea or coffee beans and then subdivide the flavors into smaller packets that you seal into a tin so the items retain their freshness. (Such a gift is probably better purchased in the late autumn.)

- *Scented guest soaps and embroidered hand towels* are gifts appropriate for any stop-by family.

- *Candles,* especially those that are carved or decorated in unusual ways, are a good gift item for both men and women.

- *Woolen neck scarves* in solid, neutral colors are a gift nearly every adult will enjoy.

- *A small stuffed animal* is a good gift to have on hand for any child from toddler to teenager. (Check on washability and safety before giving a stuffed animal to a young child or an infant.)

- Have you been given a gift that is a duplicate of something you already have? Don't have time or don't know where to exchange it? Store it away to give next year.

How to Do It   How do you discreetly disappear and reappear only moments later with your gift prepared for the giving? Have a few gift bags, colored tissue paper, and a set of generic gift tags available in the same area where you are stashing your "extra" gifts.

In purchasing these gifts, choose something that you wouldn't mind receiving. After all, if no unexpected guest shows up, you can always "gift" yourself.

42 ★ Make a Special Gift to Your Favorite Charity

Where charity stands watching
And faith holds wide the door,
The dark night wakes, the glory breaks,
And Christmas comes once more.
—O Little Town of Bethlehem

It comes as a surprise to most people to learn that December is not usually one of the better financial months for many charity groups and not-for-profit organizations. It seems that many regular contributors become too caught up in their family giving and spending to remember the organizations that are dear to their hearts, and wallets, at other times of the year.

Consider making a gift during Epiphany to a not-for-profit organization of your choosing. Do it as a special love gift "unto the Lord."

- Don't do it *because* you feel guilty.

- Don't do it *because* you want a tax write-off.

- Don't do it *because* someone else is telling you that you should.

- Don't do it *because* of the appeal in a direct-mail letter.

Do it because you want to! Make a charitable gift because you choose to do it, because it pleases you to give such a gift as a tangible expression of your love for the Baby that came to this earth on your behalf. Make your gift cheerfully, with joy in your heart, as if you are handing the gift directly to the Lord Himself.

Don't let the opinion of others sway you. Pray about where to make your gift. Pray about the amount to give. As you give, pray that those who receive your gift will use it for maximum benefit in extending the witness of the Gospel. And then, give.

A gift of money, offered in the right spirit and to an organization that is undertaking work that honors the Lord, is a gift that will bear fruit.

43 ★ Give a Gift of an Event

Then may we hope, the angelic thrones among,
To sing, redeemed, a glad triumphal song.
—Byrom

Consider giving a memory as a gift. Give the gift of an *event*. You might choose:

- *tickets to a concert,* perhaps presented in a box with a little gold filigree music stand;

- *tickets to the circus,* in a box of cracker jacks;

- *a book of tickets to a local movie theatre,* in a tin of popcorn;

- *tickets to a stage play,* in a bar of chocolate;

- *tickets to the zoo,* clutched in the hands of a small stuffed animal;

- *tickets to an ice skating exhibition,* wrapped with an ice cube tray;

- *tickets to a sporting event,* wrapped up in a sweatband or a box of white athletic socks (or any other item related to the sporting event or the team that will be playing).

Give a Trip   If you are really feeling extravagant, consider tickets that will take the recipient on a trip. Tuck them in a box with items that are appropriate to the destination—a bottle of suntan lotion, for example, for tickets to Hawaii.

I recently gave my father "airline points" for a trip to Switzerland, tucked inside a leather passport holder. (The tickets were free ones for mileage earned from business trips; the total cost of the gift was only the $20 for the passport holder!)

"Create" a Ticket

You might also "create" a ticket—using simple construction paper and your imagination—for an evening out at an elegant restaurant, a visit to a local art gallery or museum and tea afterwards, or a picnic in the park come spring.

When you give tickets as a gift, you never need to worry about fit, style, or whether the gift will be appreciated or enjoyed. You don't have to worry about calories or breakage.

When you give the gift of an event, you are giving the gift of future memories. Your gift may well last a lifetime.

When you give the gift of an event, you are projecting the Christmas spirit of love and giving out of the home setting and into the world at large. Consider Christmas giving in ticket form!

44 ★ Give a Gift of Service

What can I give him, poor as I am?
If I were a shepherd, I would bring a lamb;
If I were a Wise Man, I would do my part;
Yet what I can I give him—give my heart.
—In the Bleak Midwinter

One of the most appreciated gifts you will ever give is a gift certificate for your time and service. Strive to give a gift of service that has these three hallmarks:

1. The gift certificate should be for a service that is not already expected of you. If a child is required to rake leaves from the front lawn, a certificate for leaf raking is not a gift.
2. The gift certificate should be given so that the recipient is freed from a chore or an obligation. A gift certificate that says, "I'll help you" or "I'll work alongside you" doesn't really count. The recipient should be totally free to devote time and energy to something else.
3. The gift of service should represent a sacrifice on the part of the giver. The gift will be more valuable if it is perceived to be something difficult or time-consuming for the giver.

Suggested Service Gifts With those characteristics in mind, you may want to consider giving one of the following gifts.

- *Give child care or elder care.*

Do you know someone who is pretty much tied to home because he is the sole provider of care to an elderly person or a sick relative? Give that person a break! Give him a gift certificate of your service.

- *Give chore duty.*

A child will enjoy receiving a gift certificate from a sibling (or even a parent) for "chore relief." Chore duty gift certificates can extend beyond the family, of course. Perhaps there's a neighbor next door who needs a few small repairs made in her house but always insists on paying for even the most minor assistance. Give her a gift certificate that covers a period of hours of free home repair or the gift of labor related to a specific chore (such as installation of storm windows or window washing).

- *Give meal service.*

This is an especially appreciated gift by mothers who work outside the home. Volunteer to bring over an entire meal for her family or to cater a meal in her home. Make the event festive, including flowers and candles. You may want your gift certificate to read more like an invitation to a dinner party in her own home.

Be Specific   As you make your gift certificate, be certain to specify exactly what you are covering—the number of hours you are giving, the services you expect to render, the dates the recipient may choose to "cash in" the certificate, and so forth.

Make certain that you can do a quality job in providing

the service you expect to give. Don't undertake a job that is *normally* done by a professional.

A gift of service is truly a gift that comes from your heart *and* your hands. It is a gift of your time, energy, creativity, and helpful love.

45 ★ Give an Unheralded Gift of Your Time

At thy great name of Jesus, now
All knees must bend, all hearts must bow;
And things celestial thee shall own,
And things terrestrial, Lord alone.
—Latin Hymn

During the holiday season, when time seems to be scarce for many people, a gift of your time is a wonderful and rare gift.

Unexpected Help This is not the time for a "certificate." Just show up! Don't announce your intention; offer your help in the now moment of the season. You may, of course, give an advance call or schedule a time to help out. But, don't couch your offer of time and service in terms of a gift. Make this something for which you expect no return and no acknowledgement from others.

- Do you have a friend who you know is being swallowed up by the party plans she has made? Perhaps she has overextended or undercalculated or a child has become sick. Show up to help with an extra pair of willing hands.

- Has a neighbor broken a leg, rendering him unable to remove the snow from his driveway? Activate your shovel on his behalf, volunteer to drive him to work, or hire a neighborhood teenager to get the job done for both of you.

- Give the local homeless shelters a call. See if they need extra volunteers during the winter season. This is a great activity for the entire family. Make it your gift of service to your community.

- Is a friend at work expecting a horde of relatives? Could the host family use a few more large pots and pans or extra bed linens? Would the friend like help getting the house cleaned and decorated in advance of the guests arrival?

- Are you aware that one of your clergy has an especially busy day? Offer to be his chauffeur. Save him all the extra minutes that it often takes to find a parking space, not to mention the mental and emotional wear and tear of holiday traffic.

- Consider taking an elderly friend shopping. Arrange for a wheelchair, if appropriate, and do the pushing.

A gift of time does two things in our lives: It shifts our priorities away from ourselves and turns us outward, and it blesses someone we know or love in an unusual and unexpected way, often causing that person to have deeper spiritual reflections during the holiday season.

46 ★ Give Your Tree a Second Life

Thee, dear Lord, with heed I'll cherish;
Live to thee
Faithfully:
Dying, never perish.
            —Gerhardt

Give your cut Christmas tree another life this year. You may want to:

- Give your tree back to the environment. Watch for notices from environmental agencies in your local papers. Many trees are now weighted and positioned at the bottoms of lakes and reservoirs to provide breeding grounds for fish. As the needles fall from the trees, algae forms along the tiny branches that remain and provide a rich source of nutrients for water life.

- Give your tree to a park service. Some city and county park services welcome discarded Christmas trees, which they chop and use for mulch in city parks. Again, watch for local notices.

- Place your tree in the corner of your backyard to provide a safe winter haven for small animal wildlife.

In giving your cut tree back to the environment, you also may want to consider making a cash gift to your city park department or your local forestry office to help cover the cost of planting a tree—or several trees—to replace the one you cut from the forest.

Remember the Beauty   One year, I was especially pleased with my Christmas tree. It had been just the right size and shape, the decorations in proper proportion, and I was reluctant to discard it. So I gave that tree a second life by photographing it to use as part of a future year's Christmas card!

A friend kept her small live Christmas tree indoors until February, at which time she encouraged her children to cover it with little hearts that they had cut from construction paper and decorated with beads, lace, and glitter. "The message of Christmas is love," she said. "What better way to reinforce the Christmas theme and finish off the tree's indoor stay?"

A Community Event   You may also give your tree a second purpose, albeit a short-lived one, if your community has an Epiphany bonfire, as mine does. Trees are brought from all points of the city to a designated location well away from buildings and homes. Last year the huge pile of evergreens was more than thirty feet high. On Epiphany night, the bonfire is lit under close supervision by the local fire department. Talk about a blaze! The heat, light, and generally frigid temperatures —as well as the shimmer of sparked embers rising heavenward—make for a final burst of holiday splendor and festivity. As one person noted, "It's a way to make the holiday season go out with a bang, rather than a whimper." It certainly beats bagging a tree and sending it off to the city dump.

47 ★ Give the Gift of Words

Shout the glad tidings, exultingly sing, . . .
Jerusalem triumphs, Messiah is King!
—Muhlenberg

For your holiday greetings this season, consider sending a blank card on which you write a personal blessing. A blessing is, by definition, a statement that recognizes the hallowed, consecrated, or holy nature of the person.

You may be comfortable extending a blessing only to a few close friends or loved ones, or to those with whom you have a deep spiritual bond. Even if you only send such a message to a few people, or to many, make the effort to do so. In both your own life and theirs, you will be calling attention in a significant way to the holiness of the season.

Your message need not be a long treatise. It certainly need not be smarmy or exaggerated in emotion. Here are some suggestions:

- *"My wish for you this Epiphany, _____ [friend's name], is this: _____ [add your personalized wish]."* Your wish need not be entirely serious; it may stem from a shared experience. You might include one wish or several.

- *"My prayer for you and your family this Epiphany is . . ."* Your prayer may be one that you take from an established prayer book or a quote from a book of inspiration. It may be a Scripture passage.

- *"At this Epiphany season, I share your dreams*

for . . ." Do you know what the person is desiring in his or her life—of a spiritual or personal nature? Let the person know that you are one in spirit with him or her.

- *"My word to you for this Epiphany season is . . ."* Focus on one word. In fact, you don't even need the prelude. A few years ago, after a particularly difficult emotional trauma, I received a beautiful holiday card from a friend. It had baroque angels in abundance on the front of the card and only one handwritten word as an interior message: "Strength." The card held much meaning for me. Indeed, my strength during that period came from "on high" and from such loving friends as the sender of that card.

    You may want to use one word, several words, or even the entire list of Spirit-given attributes found in Galatians 5:22–23: love, joy, peace, longsuffering, kindness, goodness, faithfulness, gentleness, self-control.

- *"May the blessings of the Lord fill your life this Epiphany . . ."* You may state specific blessings that you believe are pertinent to that person or more general ones that you draw from Scriptures. Any Bible verse that conveys a promise is a good one to share. Or, you may simply call attention to the fact that as a believer in the Lord Jesus, the recipient of your card *is* blessed!

One season I received a card that said simply, "Blessed are you among women. Never forget it." I never have.

You may want to write a poem or a prose statement of

blessing, decorate it, and laminate it to make a Bible bookmark. Your greeting will have a longer life.

A greeting of heartfelt words only takes an extra minute or two for each person or family on your list. The message conveyed, however, is likely to be one that lodges more deeply, lives more potently, and lasts far longer in the soul of the one who receives it.

48 ★ Remember Those Who Must Serve Us All During the Holiday Season

Though an infant now we view him,
He shall fill his Father's throne,
Gather all the nations to him,
Every knee shall then bow down.
                    —Angels, from the Realm of Glory

The Baby born in Bethlehem came to serve, to "gather all nations round him," and it is because He lived a life of service and sacrifice that we worship Him today.

The Four M's Epiphany is a time for remembering in a special way those who serve us all, and especially those who served without respite during the holiday season, even on Christmas Eve and Christmas Day. I refer to them as the "Four M's."

- *Ministers*—who lead worship services and are available twenty-four hours a day to those in their parishes who are sick, dying, grieving, or in need. Consider all who assist the homeless, abused, disoriented, or impoverished as "ministers."

- *Military personnel*—who defend our nation and its

principles at home and abroad, even to the sacrifice of their own lives.

- *Medical personnel*—who walk the hallways of our nation's hospitals, respond to accidents, and give their life-saving service in emergencies.

- *Municipal servants*—who keep the peace, protect our property, fight our fires, and do their utmost to assure our safety so that we might truly enjoy a prosperous season.

Unseen People   Each of us is surrounded by a host of unseen people who are on duty preserving the way of life and the quality of life we have come to accept as normal. Epiphany is an ideal time to thank them in a special way.

- Show up at your local fire or police station with a tin of cookies or a box of candy.

- Write a letter to the editor of your local newspaper thanking the "Four M's" in your community for their dedicated service during the holidays.

- Send a Christmas card to your sheriff's office. And to the police precinct or highway patrol office nearest you. And to the firehouse that serves your neighborhood.

- If you're a student, drop a note of thanks to your campus security department.

- Make a special donation to your local hospital.

- Send a plant to the nurses who took care of you

during your surgery last spring. Let them know that you are still thankful for their care and appreciative of the fact that they are always willing to serve.

- Mail cards, cookies, or tapes to military personnel. You can send a packet to "Any Soldier" if you don't know someone personally. He or she will appreciate your thoughtfulness.

As you send your card or make your gift, add a note of appreciation. *"Thank you for serving. May your New Year be an extra special one."*

49 ★ Don't Overspend

Vainly we offer each ample oblation,
Vainly with gifts would his favor secure;
Richer by far is the heart's adoration,
Dearer to God are the prayers of the poor.
—Heber

The frenzy of purchasing and the subsequent onslaught of credit card invoices leave many shoppers with feelings of exhaustion and overextension, not to mention downright dismay and debt.

Set a budget now for next Christmas. Plan to purchase your gifts all through the year to even out the financial burden. Make a resolution not to put Christmas purchases on credit cards. All of these methods will help you keep spending within reasonable limits.

Gifts Under $5 Strive to keep your gifts simple and lasting in nature. Consider the abundance of charming and meaningful gifts that you might give at a cost of under $5. (Yes, it *is* possible to give a nice gift that costs so little!)

- Turn blooms from your garden into potpourri and give a clear plastic box of them to a friend. Include a small vial of scented oil.

- Enlarge a favorite photo to 4″ × 6″ or 5″ × 7″ size and cut a double mat for it. Wrap it tightly in saran wrap. (Many people prefer to choose their own frames anyway!)

- Box together an assortment of six votive candles in green, red, and white—scented, if possible.

- Braid together strands of narrow velvet ribbon to create an avant-garde bracelet or belt.

- Embroider a handkerchief.

- Trim a small basket with ribbon and fill it with an assortment of gift soaps.

- Early in the fall, start rooting some cuttings from your houseplants. Pot them in unusual containers for gifting.

- Browse through flea markets, antique stores, secondhand bookstores, and garage sales for unusual items at bargain prices.

- Look through your own home for items that may have heirloom quality for a niece, nephew, adult child, or grandchild.

- Sew clothes for a child's favorite doll. Use scraps of material left over from previous projects.

- Fill a small decorative jar or container with M&M's candy or jelly beans for a coworker's desk.

The list of inexpensive items is virtually endless. Plan to give gifts that say you have invested your time, thought, and creativity.

50 ★ Make Your Thank You Notes Meaningful

Sacred gifts of mystic meaning;
Incense doth their God disclose.
Gold the King of kings proclaimeth,
Myrrh his sepulchre foreshows.
—Prudentius

I have a hunch the wise men didn't know the symbolic meaning behind their gifts. Certainly they knew they were bringing gifts of great value—gold, frankincense, and myrrh were rare treasures in the ancient world. These were gifts worthy of royalty, which is precisely what the Magi were seeking.

We have no indication, however, apart from their gifts, that the wise men were coming to honor a *spiritual king* (with gold), a *priest* (with the incense of frankincense for worship), or a *prophet* (with the embalming ointment for his future fate as a prophet). As foreigners, Jesus most certainly would not have been *their* prophet, priest, and king at that time, even if they recognized those qualities as definitive of His life!

The gifts you receive, to a great extent, may well be meaningful to you in ways that the recipient never intended. What a nice surprise for the gift-giver when you see those "hidden" meanings and share them in your thank-you note.

- Has a friend or relative given you a gift of cologne or aftershave or some other scented personal product? *"Your friendship is a sweet fragrance in my life. Thank you for this gift to remind me of that fact!"*

- Have you been given a lovely or practical gift for your home? *"Thank you for helping make my home a place of welcome."*

- Have you been given something that is alive, perhaps a plant or a pet? *"Life is precious in all forms, and your life is certainly precious to me. Thank you for being in mine."*

By seeing another dimension in a gift, you are riveting your own attention, as well as that of the gift-giver, back to the fact that behind all the outward show and activity of the holiday season, friendships are invaluable.

51 ★ Frame Your New Year's Resolutions in Terms of Giving

We wish you a Merry Christmas
And a happy New Year.
　　　　　—We Wish You a Merry Christmas

Adopt a "giving" mindset as you map out your resolutions for the coming year. Among the many dictionary definitions for the word *resolution,* one recently stood out to me in a new way: "to reduce to simpler form." Often, we tend to make too many resolutions. Try concentrating on just one resolution for change in your life.

- *What is the* one *change that would bring your life more sharply into focus this coming year?*

- *What is the* one *essential that you desire in your life?*

- *What is your* top *priority?*

- *What is your* supreme *goal or challenge?*

- *What is the* foremost *gift that you desire from the Lord this year?*

Choose that *one* thing as the basis for your resolution. Seek to be single-minded in your approach to the New Year. Ask yourself, "When all is said and done, what will really matter?" Channel your energies and your coming days toward that end.

Discernment The Latin root for our English word *resolution* speaks of discernment. It is important that we seek to discern God's best for our lives. It is critical that we blanket our New Year's resolution with prayer. Ask the heavenly Father to help you see His purposes for your life, discover His desires for you, unearth the ways in which He would seek for you to grow and become more like His Son.

The Greek word for *resolution* relates to the concepts of "choosing" or "deciding." Your resolution must be rooted deeply in your will. If not, your resolution is really just a wish or a daydream. What is it that you are truly willing to devote your physical strength, ideas, and emotional energy toward doing or accomplishing?

Consider rooting all your resolutions in the central concept of *giving*. What do you resolve to give to the Lord during the coming year? Think in terms of your time, ability, finances, creativity. What can you do to extend His kingdom, to bring joy to His heart, to share His good news with others?

What do you resolve to give to yourself during this coming year? Yes, *you!* Don't forget to give to yourself. Acknowledge yourself as worthy of God's greatest gift, and therefore, worthy of your own greatest gifts. Consider new ways to give yourself the gifts of forgiveness, health, and joy.

What do you resolve to give to those around you? How better might you share your life with them? God's gift of His Son to you is a gift that He intends for you to pass along to others. Chart a means for doing so.

52 ★ Don't Expect More than the Holidays Can Give

And thus that manger poor
Became a throne;
For he whom Mary bore
Was God the son.
—Venite Adoremus

Think back over all of your favorite holiday memories. What really stands out when subjected to the test of time?

It is probably not the gifts you have received. I suspect that you can't recall all that you received as presents the year you were eight years old. In fact, I suspect that you can't recall vividly more than a dozen gifts that you received throughout your entire childhood. Try listing those things that you received just last year! No . . . the central fact of Christmas is not to be found in the exchange of presents.

It is probably not the events in which you have participated, although those experiences may be more easily and vividly recalled. The beauty, meaning, and feeling of special moments often fade fairly quickly. We often remember only that we went or did—not the details of the experience. It is difficult to recapture the intensity of feelings once felt. Even family reunions tend to blur in memory. Can you recall *all* the faces that were at your holiday party last year?

It is probably not even the quiet holy moments that you have spent in meditation. Those experiences and their resultant insights often tend to weave themselves into the total fabric of our lives in a way that leaves them indistinguishable and incapable of being isolated.

So what is it that lodges so deeply in our memory that it cannot be erased by time?

I am convinced that relationships are the heart of the holidays.

- It's the reason God sent His Son as a baby—so that we might have a *relationship* with Him.

- It's the reason we give gifts—to build *relationships*.

- It's the reason we plan holiday reunions and parties —to allow for the growth of *relationships* and give us an opportunity to share moments of joy with those we love.

Perhaps any disappointment we feel comes down to misplaced priorities. We have looked to presents or decorations or parties to provide us with joy, when in fact, only relationships have the potential to truly satisfy and enrich.

Don't expect the holidays, per se, to provide something that they can't. Do expect to have to reach out in love to others and to embrace openly the outstretched arms of affection extended toward you, including the outstretched loving arms of the heavenly Father Himself.

When all of the visitors have gone home, the wrappings have been discarded, the journals have been shelved, and the decorations have been put away for another year, this fact remains: God gives to us His Child—nearly two thousand years ago and again every year—and our *relationship* with Him is all that ultimately matters.